TD

7.26.78

How to Buy a Home

How to Buy a Home

a practical guide to finding and buying the right home

Connie Fletcher

Consultant—Robert G. Walters,
Senior Vice President,
Baird & Warner Inc.

  78 18154 3

FOLLETT PUBLISHING COMPANY
Chicago

Edited by Susan David.

Copyright ©1978 by Follett Publishing Company, a division of
Follett Corporation. All rights reserved. No portion of this book
may be used or reproduced in any manner whatsoever without
written permission from the publisher except in the case of brief
quotations embodied in critical reviews and articles. Manufac-
tured in the United States of America.

Library of Congress Cataloging in Publication Data

Fletcher, Connie, 1947–
  How to buy a home.

  1. House buying—Handbooks, manuals, etc. I. Title.
TH4817.5.F58 643 77-19298
ISBN 0-695-80884-2

Contents

2023699

Introduction

The decision to buy a home is an important one. Like choosing what kind of work you will do, it can affect the rest of your life. So it is important that you give a good deal of thought and attention to choosing the home that is right for you.

You can make a worthwhile choice, one that will more than repay you in financial and psychological benefits, if you look carefully before you buy. You could make a costly mistake, though, if you fail to learn beforehand all you can about finding and buying a home.

The Benefits of Home Ownership

Buying a home can be one of the most important investments you make in your own future. The financial benefits alone are worth considering. Here are some sound reasons for owning a home.

- Home ownership is a good way to keep ahead of inflation. Although almost everything else you may buy now—automobiles, TV sets, refrigerators, and so on—starts depreciating, or lessening in value, as soon as you buy it, your home may not. Property values actually rise during times of inflation. During the last few years property values have risen much faster and farther than anything else in the general economy.

- Owning your own home is a sound investment. Most likely your property will increase in value, and you will be able to sell it for a profit. If you have a mortgage, or loan, on your home, each payment on the mortgage adds something to the money value you have in the home, or your equity. Your equity is the cash difference between the market value of your home and the amount you still owe on your mortgage. While this share may be small for some time, your growing equity, along with the increasing value of your home, means a safe, steady investment for you.

- Home ownership can also mean savings on income taxes. You can deduct both real estate taxes and the interest you pay on your mortgage from your federal income tax and from income tax in some states. Some settlement costs that you pay when you purchase your home are also deductible. If you sell your home at a profit, you can put off paying taxes on the profit if you reinvest in another home of any greater value within eighteen months of the sale.

- Owning a home improves your credit rating.

- Your mortgage payments can serve as proof of credit for any emergency loan you may need.

What a Home Can Mean in Your Life

Owning a home has great financial advantages. But if you're considering buying, you're probably even more excited about the *idea* of having your own home. There are some things that only a home can provide. For example:

- A home of your own can give you and your family a feeling of security.
- You have more room and more privacy in your own house.
- A home can offer stability in our fast-changing world.
- A house, which often offers more living space and outdoor privacy than an apartment, is an excellent environment for raising children.
- If you own your home, you are free to make any alterations of house and grounds within the limits of your imagination, pocketbook, and the local zoning requirements.

Warning: Hunt with Care

While owning a home can be a fine investment and a rewarding experience, you may meet with some hazards. You may end up with a home that doesn't really satisfy your needs and those of your family. You may get in over your head financially or be faced with unforeseen expenses. You may decide too quickly on a home only to find the "perfect" home too late.

Buying your own home is a big commitment. There are many technical questions involved that concern both the home itself and how to pay for it. This book is designed to take the guesswork and risks out of buying a home. Before you even start your hunt for a home, you should know what to look for and what to avoid in locations, structures, and methods of financing.

How to Buy a Home deals with everything from air vents to zoning regulations. Therefore, this book can help you answer these all-important questions:

- What kinds of homes are currently available?
- How much should I pay for a home?
- How can I arrange financing for my home?
- How do I start house-hunting?
- How do I find a real estate broker or agent?
- How can I judge the quality of a house?
- What should I look for in a neighborhood?
- What are the best methods of protecting and maintaining my home?

If you study and use this guide, you should find buying your home both profitable and fun.

1
What Should You Buy?

The first step in intelligent home buying is knowing what choices you have. After considering your special needs and tastes, you'll be able to decide what kind of home is right for you.

In today's market, you can choose from several kinds of ownership and types of homes. You may want to buy your own house, or you may be interested in a condominium or a cooperative. Detached houses, for either single-family or multifamily units, are available. So are town houses and mobile homes. You can buy an old home and renovate it, purchase a new home, or contract for your home to be built according to your specifications.

All these options in home buying can become confusing. This chapter lays out the advantages and disadvantages of each possible choice of ownership and type of home. As you hunt for a home, jot down in a notebook your impressions of each kind of home you look at. Also note all the facts you discover, including the price of the home, the name of the owner, the real estate taxes, the number of bedrooms and bathrooms, the type of utilities (such as gas or electric heat), and any special features.

Which Type of Ownership?

INDIVIDUAL OWNERSHIP

The traditional way to own a home is to purchase the home, property, and equipment yourself—to own it lock, stock, and barrel. This individual ownership plan is a major commitment in time and expense. When you consider this type of ownership, you must keep in mind the size of your family, your current and estimated future income, and whether or not you expect to move again.

When you buy a home, you obtain the *title* to the real estate property. The American Bar Association defines the title to real estate as "the right of the owner to its peaceful possession and use, free from the claims of others." You gain the right to occupy your home without interference. You also have the right to sell or to mortgage your home whenever you wish to in the future.

However, under individual ownership, your use of your property may be restricted in some ways. For example, you may meet with local governmental zoning laws or restrictions in the deed, the legal document that transfers ownership. Almost all land is subject to general property taxes. If you fail to pay these taxes, you could lose the title to your property. Very often if specific property improvements have been made in your area, such as improved streets or a new sewer system, you may be charged a special tax.

You should examine all such restrictions carefully before you buy your home; you may find that what seems to be a desirable home in light of mortgage payments is otherwise impossible for you to handle financially.

Individual home ownership brings with it many responsibilities. You're responsible, first of all, for the upkeep of house and grounds. As an owner of a house, part of your mortgage agreement is that you'll keep the property in good condition. For example, you must keep the sidewalks by your house safely paved and free from ice and snow. Keeping your house in order is not only an asset to your neighborhood but makes sound financial sense in case you decide to sell it at some future time.

A word of caution: Unless you're a natural fix-it type, you may run into trouble if you try to repair some equipment and appliances yourself. You may even void the warranty on some equipment if you botch a repair job. So, for more than minor repairs, first consult the builder or supplier of the equipment under warranty for repairs. After the warranty expires, hire an expert or become one yourself.

Individual ownership can involve considerable financial responsibilities. Property taxes, insurance, heat and other utilities, maintenance, and repair costs are just some of the expenses home ownership demands.

Financing Your Home. Since home ownership requires long-range financing, your personal finances (including your ability to budget and to estimate your future income) are of prime importance. Consider the following factors well before you decide on individual home ownership.

- How much of your income can you set aside for housing costs?
- What cash reserves do you have available?
- What are your future financial prospects?
  Your present income is the first indicator of what

you can afford in a home. But when you estimate how much of your present income can be used for housing, also take into account how any changes in your income or that of your spouse would affect you. If you buy your home with a mortgage, remember that your housing allowance must cover monthly mortgage payments *and* all other expenses involved in owning a home.

The next consideration for owning a home is the extent of your cash reserves. You need cash for a down payment on a home, for closing costs, for moving expenses, and for any decorating or improvement costs involved in setting up your home. Your cash reserves also act as an emergency fund for any unforeseen repair expenses that may come up.

Finally, your own financial future is an important factor in whether or not you buy a home. Depending upon how secure or happy you are in your present job, what the advancement picture at work looks like, and whether or not you expect to be transferred, you can either buy a house or investigate other home-ownership options for the time being.

The Tax Picture. As an individual homeowner, you must pay real estate taxes. You may also have to pay the special assessment tax for a specific property improvement mentioned earlier. In some areas, the home buyer must pay taxes on the exchange of property.

Property taxes are not fixed and may vary in different parts of the country. The current owner of the home or a real estate professional can give you an estimate of annual property taxes, but, because taxes are so changeable, double-check these figures against office records of the city or county assessor.

Although the tax estimates may seem discouraging, remember that tax benefits are part of the plus side of owning your own home. State and local property taxes are deductible from your federal income tax, as are interest payments on a mortgage. Real estate taxes are deductible only in the year they are paid to the government. These tax benefits for home ownership can mean long-range savings for you. They also tend to lower the cost of owning a home.

Insurance Costs. Property insurance is a necessary expense in home ownership. As a buyer, you're required to carry enough insurance to cover the amount of your mortgage. Insurance usually covers the replacement cost of the home, a safeguard in case of property destruction. You should periodically review your coverage to make sure you are carrying enough insurance.

Since insurance can be costly, it's important not to overinsure your home. No insurance company can pay more than the replacement cost of any damage. Also, don't buy the first policy you come across. There are many types of insurance to choose from. Fire insurance protects you against any damage to your home resulting from fire or lightning. You may want a fire insurance policy with extended coverage to protect against damage caused by hailstorms, tornadoes, wind, explosions, aircraft, a vehicle, and smoke. Personal liability insurance offers you protection in case someone is injured on your property; this coverage extends to injuries or damages suffered by your family. Theft insurance, which is available in both limited and broad coverage, protects your personal property against robbery, burglary, and larceny. Package policies are available, too, in the form of a homeowners' policy. Such a policy combines property and personal property insurance with personal liability insurance and is often cheaper than insurance coverage bought separately. To find out about current costs and collection procedures, consult a qualified insurance agent. Be sure to examine the various kinds of insurance before you buy.

All the factors discussed—home upkeep, the amount of your savings, taxes you must pay, and insurance policies you must carry—should figure in your decision on whether or not ownership of a house is your best bet right now. They determine if you can afford the time and the money for individual ownership. An important consideration that should not be overlooked, however, is how you feel about the security, roots, and commitment represented by your own house.

THE COOPERATIVE

Two alternatives to individual home ownership have become very popular—the cooperative and the condominium. The cooperative or condominium style of ownership combines some of the advantages of owning a house with the advantages of renting an apartment. It's important to understand the difference between cooperatives and condominiums in terms of benefits and responsibilities.

If you join a cooperative, you are part of a group of people who have bought a building and who share in the building's success. The group buys a building; there is one mortgage and one tax bill. Individual members of the cooperative are responsible for making payments toward meeting the mortgage and tax expenses and maintaining the structure. An individual shares in a housing corporation and owns a share of stock or a membership certificate in the total enterprise and holds either a perpetual lease or a ninety-nine-year lease on his or her own dwelling.

Besides owning a share in the cooperative project, you share in the liabilities of the building. For example, if one cooperative member fails to pay his or her share of the taxes or defaults on his or her payment toward the mortgage, the responsibility is held by the building as a whole. The other members must make good on the obligation.

Cooperative responsibility is most like the responsibility you undertake when you rent an apartment; that is, although you do not own your living quarters, you are responsible for keeping walls, floors, and home appliances in good, workable condition. You must also pay for the repair of any internal damages your individual living unit may suffer.

Financing a cooperative is both personal and communal, or by the group. Individual occupants pay for their living quarters. You will also pay monthly charges for the building's maintenance, for cooperative real estate taxes and financing, and for stockholder obligations.

The great advantage to cooperative living is that you have a prorated share, or a share figured from your particular financial contribution, in the success of the total project. If the property has increased in value and the ownership decides to sell, you will make a profit on your investment. It's like living in an apartment or town house and also being part owner of the building itself. This advantage carries with it certain responsibilities, however, such as personal upkeep and responsibility for the other shareholders.

These obligations must be fully weighed before you decide upon cooperative ownership.

See chapter 10 for a more detailed discussion of cooperatives.

THE CONDOMINIUM

If you buy into a condominium, you own a home in a multiunit building. Usually these buildings are apartment complexes or town houses. Condominiums are gaining in variety as well as popularity. They range from expensive sites near oceans or golf courses to quite reasonably priced apartments or town houses.

Owning a condominium is different from owning a house. When you buy a condominium, you own the inner living space of the dwelling (the space between the four walls, floor, and ceiling). When you buy a house, you own the inner space plus the exterior and grounds of the house. If you live in a condominium, you and your neighbors jointly own the grounds and exterior facilities, such as the parking lot and the recreation area, and maintain them through a co-owners' association. Unlike the owner of a cooperative, the condominium owner has no obligation for any other condominium owner's mortgage or tax payments.

One of the advantages of condominium living is that you can enjoy the grounds and use the recreation areas without having to mow the lawn, clean the swimming pool, or rake the tennis courts yourself. The management of the condominium must handle the maintenance of the building, although the condominium owners pay for this service. However, you must take care of your own private dwelling.

The financial responsibilities attached to condominium living are both personal and communal, as in cooperatives. You must provide your own fire, personal property, and liability insurance. You must meet payments on your own home. You are responsible for local real estate taxes on your dwelling.

As part of the condominium community, you must pay a monthly fee to finance maintenance operations such as trash collection, repairs, lawn care, snow removal, and upkeep of any recreational facilities.

See chapter 10 for more information on condominiums.

What Kind of Home Suits You?

Before you hunt for a home, be aware that homes come in all shapes, sizes, styles, and prices. Don't confine yourself to one type of structure. You may find that a far different home would be a better buy and a better living arrangement for you.

The detached house, on its own lot, has several advantages. First, you're able to enjoy your own yard. Second, you may own your own garage or carport. Detached houses generally offer more living space than apartments do. Finally, detached houses come in a wide variety of styles.

Town houses are usually priced lower than single-family homes, but they offer several of the same life-style and financial benefits. Town houses can be one-, two-, or three-story structures; the most common type of town house is the two-story unit. Town house owners must pay their own taxes and insurance. Many town house complexes come equipped with swimming pool, clubhouses, and other recreational facilities.

Another housing alternative is the apartment. Apartments are as varied as houses. You can choose among high rises, courtyard buildings, smaller buildings, or even old homes divided into apartments. High rises can afford a sense of security, since many have guards and electronic screening equipment. The view from a high rise can be spectacular. Smaller apartments can be cozy and comfortable. Your decision to live in a house or an apartment should be based on an awareness of what you want from a living space and how much you want to pay for it.

The mobile home has undergone tremendous improvements since it was first introduced. Mobile homes are no longer spartan living units but are often convenient and elegant—and easily financed. Since more manufacturers are producing mobile homes that meet building code standards, longer-term conventional mortgages can now be obtained for mobile homes. This represents a financial step-up for the mobile home owner.

Whatever type of home you buy, its age is an important consideration. It can affect you primarily in terms of how many repair bills you pay. Here, as with every aspect of home buying, you must set aside all assumptions until you've had a chance to really explore every type of home. Don't be dazzled by a home just because it's new; on the other hand, don't confuse age with solid worth. Size up each home on its own merits.

THE OLD HOME

Any home that has been lived in before, whether for generations or for only a year, is known in real estate terms as an "existing" or "used" home. Older homes have much going for them. Usually the neighborhood surrounding an older home is established, making it easier for you to judge the convenience of shopping centers, churches or synagogues, schools, and transportation. If you favor unique, individual architecture, an older home might satisfy your sense of beauty. Older homes can be utterly charming, equipped with style refinements not available today.

Old homes also offer more space for the money than new homes. Ceiling heights, floor space, and room sizes are generally on a grander scale than in newly built homes or apartments.

Buying an older home can also make sound financial sense. Because of the growing demand for antique or renovated homes, you may make a considerable profit on the resale price.

There can be drawbacks to owning an older home, however. The major problem is often the condition of the home. You may buy a home without being informed or aware of any defects, such as breakdown of the furnace, deficient plumbing, or flooding problems in the basement. As homes get older, problems with wiring, heating, and plumbing usually increase. Renovation can sometimes prove more expensive and time-consuming than it's worth.

Another thing to remember is that if there is an existing mortgage on the house you are considering, it must be paid off before the house can ever become yours. The seller is responsible for this payment if he or she is delivering a property free from other claims. You can either get a mortgage of your own or you can take on the original mortgage of the seller. If you *do* decide to assume the mortgage of the former owner, the mortgage lender for that particular home must approve of you. Consult an attorney to make sure of your financing arrangements before you commit yourself to buying an older home.

THE NEW HOME

Moving into a home never before lived in can be a very satisfying experience. And it has definite advantages. To begin with, a new home is in top condition. With your home, you get new plumbing, heating, and wiring units. You may receive a builder's warranty, which binds the builder to fix anything that needs repair within the first year. Second, your property insurance rates may be lower than for a used home because the wiring and heating systems have not deteriorated yet.

But there are some potential pitfalls in ownership of a new home. You must be careful to inspect and judge the quality of the structure itself. Ignorance about construction flaws or site mistakes can lead to expensive maintenance and repair jobs later on. You may suffer a dwindling profit on any future resale because you've paid top dollar for your new home.

THE HOME THAT'S NOT YET BUILT

Perhaps you don't want to buy an already existing structure. You want to share in the entire project yourself, so you contract to have your home built.

This method of home construction can be fascinating and extremely rewarding. You're able to watch your home grow from the foundation up. You have the advantage of being able to check out the construction process at every stage and prevent or alter features before they become permanent.

At the same time, building a home presents a special set of difficulties.

- How well are you able to judge the quality of construction?
- How can you determine the reliability of your builder?
- How can you communicate your ideas on construction and changes you may want made?
- Is there a way you can estimate the total cost of construction?
- How soon must you be able to move in?

Whatever type of home and terms of ownership you decide upon, remember that being well informed in advance is your best defense against rip-offs and disappointments.

2

What Should You Pay
for Your Home?

You've decided that you want to buy or build a home. You've thought about family size and needs, types of ownership, and the kind of home that appeals to you.

But you're nowhere near your goal of home ownership until you figure out how much you can afford to pay for a home and how you can go about financing your home.

When you estimate your financial status, don't just think in terms of how much the house itself will cost. You must also bear in mind the total housing expense—operating and maintenance costs, mortgage and tax payments, and insurance expenses. You are not finished with your home buying at the time of purchase—the financial commitment extends over years.

How Do You Get a Loan?

The usual way of buying a home is to make a down payment at the time of purchase and then make monthly mortgage payments. Hardly anyone pays in full for a home these days. Most people rely on mortgage loans to help them finance the home.

A mortgage loan is a contract in which you, the buyer, pledge your home as security for a loan that is repaid in installments over a period of time. The contract states the amount of the loan, the interest rate, the size of the payments, and how often you make payments.

Three types of mortgage loans are currently available:

- Conventional loans
- FHA loans (insured by the Federal Housing Administration)
- VA loans (insured by the Veterans Administration)

All of these mortgage loans can be obtained in the same way. You go to a private lending institution—a bank, mortgage company, mutual savings bank, or savings and loan association—and ask to see a mortgage loan officer. Tell the officer about the home you are considering, and, if the lending institution is interested in that type of home in that location, the officer will give you a loan application. The institution will run a credit and reference check on you and appraise the home. Once this screening process is finished, you will be told whether your application for a mortgage loan has been approved. The same procedure applies if you are planning to build a home. Discuss the type of home you want to build and the location of the property with the mortgage loan officer.

Most mortgages are amortized loans. When you have an amortized loan, you must make a fixed regular payment, usually monthly, to reduce the amount that you have borrowed.

It's wise to shop around for the right mortgage, just as you shop around for the right home. You may be able to get more favorable financing—smaller monthly payments, a longer-term mortgage, a lower interest rate, or a larger loan—from another lending institution.

If you buy a used home, you may be able to take over the previous owner's mortgage. Under this arrangement, the seller of the home grants you the title to the property, and you become responsible for paying off the mortgage. The down payment requirement can be much higher than usual because you are paying the seller of the home for his or her equity. But if much of the principal has been paid, your monthly payments will be lower, and you will therefore owe less interest. You may also benefit from lower interest payments if the house was bought when interest rates were lower.

What Type of Mortgage Should You Get?

The good news in home buying is that in the past few years, the average size of down payments has gone down considerably. There is, however, still a wide range in the amounts required. The necessary cash deposit can range from virtually nothing under a VA-guaranteed mortgage to a 5 to 30 or even 40 percent down payment for an older home with a conventional mortgage. Down payments vary according to the type of mortgage you receive and the policies of the lending institutions in your area.

Let's examine each of the types of loans listed above to see how each affects the size of your down payment.

THE CONVENTIONAL LOAN

A conventional mortgage is usually obtained through a bank, savings and loan association, or insurance company. A smaller group of lenders are noninstitutional. These are individuals, groups, and companies who make mortgage loan investments but who are not required to conform to state and federal banking laws. Noninstitutional lenders' investment funds are usually made available through real estate and mortgage brokers. The mortgage terms are made between you (the mortgagor) and the lender (the mortgagee). Down payments change according to market conditions and vary with the lending institution. Generally, though, a down payment is about one-fifth of the home's purchase price.

How large should your down payment be? The advantage of making a high down payment is that it cuts down on your monthly payments for interest and principal. But there are several disadvantages to high down payments.

- A high down payment does not allow you to use your savings for other purposes, such as investments, stocks and bonds, or emergencies.
- Because your interest is tax-deductible, you lose some of your tax benefits if you make a high down payment.
- If you make a high down payment and then sell your home, your return on cash investment will be lower than if you had put less money down.

Many real estate professionals advise that the buyer try to make as small a down payment as possible.

THE FHA MORTGAGE

The Federal Housing Administration insures the lender against loss due to nonpayment by the borrower. This insurance makes it easier for families who do not have substantial savings to obtain mortgages through a private lending institution. The FHA loan generally permits smaller down payments, lower monthly payments, and longer periods to pay, extending as long as thirty to thirty-five years in some cases. The FHA sets a ceiling on the mortgage interest rate (the current rate is 8.5 percent) and will insure mortgages up to $60,000 for a single-family home. The home buyer must pay an FHA insurance premium of approximately 0.5 percent per month, which is not tax-deductible.

FHA loans do take some time to obtain. Like the conventional loans described above, FHA loans are subject to appraisal of the home. Conventional loans, however, are easier to find and arrange for.

THE VA MORTGAGE

The Veterans Administration also insures loans. It guarantees repayment of 60 percent of the unpaid amount of the loan. The GI loan program has made it possible for many veterans to finance their homes through private lenders. Veterans of the U.S. armed forces are under no time limits after their period of service has ended in obtaining the loan. Private lending institutions are more likely to approve such loans because the Veterans Administration guarantees part of the loan.

If a veteran wishes to obtain the VA mortgage loan guarantee, all he or she must do is provide a certificate of eligibility from the VA. There is no premium charge for the guarantee of a VA loan, but there is a service charge. Often no down payment is required. The VA does not require one if the purchase price of the home is lower than or the same as the appraised value of the home. The lending institution involved may still require a down payment in some cases and will follow the FHA formulas for down payments. Usually, however, the VA guaranteed loan carries the advantage of requiring no down payment on a home.

Figuring Your Financial Guidelines

When you buy a home, you need to determine two things—whether you can afford the down payment and the other expenses related to the purchase, and whether you can meet the monthly mortgage payments.

It's fairly easy to figure the down payment that you can afford. That is discussed later in this chapter. Estimating the monthly payment, however, can give you problems.

The monthly payment that you will owe the mortgage lender is based on how much money you have borrowed, what the interest rate is, and how many years have been suggested to pay off the loan.

The traditional guide to home payments is that your total monthly payment for housing should not be more than one week's gross salary. And the purchase price of a home should not exceed two and a half times your gross annual income. Many experts today suggest that because inflation can cause the cost of living to rise and more money may be needed for daily necessities, you should be more frugal in figuring the purchase price and scale it down to around

1.8 or 2 times your annual income. In estimating what you think you can afford to pay for a home, you should take into account your job security and prospects for advancement. You should also consider any income that you may have other than salary, including stock dividends and savings interest.

How do you estimate payment expenses if you've never owned a home before? Take the following steps.

1. Figure your net average monthly pay—your income *minus* regular withholdings and deductions for Social Security, taxes, retirement, and so on.
2. Estimate your average monthly expenses for nonhousing items, including food, clothing, insurance, savings, health care, transportation, entertainment, car expenses, gifts, contributions to charity, and miscellaneous expenses.
3. Subtract these monthly nonhousing expenses from your average net monthly income. The remainder is what you can comfortably afford for housing based upon your current expenses.

Figuring expenses ahead of time can be a very valuable aid both in looking for a home and for a mortgage. The checklist on the next page may help you arrive at a good estimate.

How Much Down Payment Can You Afford?

Now that you know approximately how much is necessary to make a down payment on a home, the

Checklist for
Your Monthly Housing Allowance

	EXPENSES
Food	_____
Clothing	_____
Transportation	_____
Car expenses	_____
Life insurance	_____
Health insurance	_____
Medical and dental care	_____
Education (current and future costs)	_____
Installment payments	_____
Savings	_____
Entertainment and recreation	_____
Vacations	_____
Charity	_____
Pocket money	_____
Emergency funds	_____
Other	_____
TOTAL	_____

	INCOME
Monthly net income	_____
Other sources	_____
TOTAL	_____

Subtract monthly expenses _____ from monthly income _____ . The remainder _____ is your monthly housing allowance.

next step is figuring out how you can get the necessary funds together. Consider your resources. They might include

- savings on hand
- projected savings over the next few months
- checking account
- sale of prior home
- cash value in insurance policy
- family loan
- personal note
- sale of securities

When you add these resources, you get your total buying power.

What you have in the bank in savings and checking accounts is your first and most important resource. If your savings are not enough, you may want to borrow additional funds. Be careful, however, not to overborrow. Don't make the mistake of scraping together enough money for a home that, in the long run, you can't afford. Be realistic in your estimates. Remember that unexpected costs can come up and that your income can be reduced. Do not put every available dollar into housing.

Next, estimate how much you'll have to pay in additional costs related to buying a home. You'll have to pay for

- property appraisal, the evaluation of property to determine its market value (This may be covered in the service charge for the mortgage.)
- having the title recorded
- initial mortgage payment
- prorated, or proportionately divided, taxes for remainder of the year

- attorney's fee
- insurance premium(s)
- title insurance

These expenses may vary, but they are unavoidable when buying a home. The legal processes establish your rights over the property, and the insurance will safeguard your purchase. You should consult your real estate agent or lender on the fees listed above before you sign a purchase agreement.

In buying a home, some expenses are not required but are difficult to avoid. Movers' costs can be a big expense. You may want to do some rebuilding or make major decorating changes in your new home. Get estimates on these before you're strapped with a huge bill. You may want to replace home appliances. Again, figure these costs before you commit yourself to spending more than you can afford.

Take all these expense figures, including everything from professional fees to household appliances, and subtract them from your cash supply. The remainder should give you a fair idea of what kind of down payment is in your range.

Escrow

Many lending institutions will require you to set up an escrow account. This is a fund to which you contribute regularly so that your real estate taxes and hazard insurance are sure to be paid. As a new homeowner, you will suddenly be called upon to pay these and other expenses. Since not all homeowners are entirely prepared to handle these costs, the lender wants an escrow account established in order to protect his or her investment.

This benefits you in several ways. The lender takes care of all the headaches and paperwork for you. Your bills are paid on time, and unexpected expenses won't force you to do additional borrowing just to meet your bills.

Since you do not usually get any interest on your escrow account, you may feel your money could be put to better use elsewhere. But for most families, especially those operating on a shoestring budget, an escrow account is advisable.

Your Long-Range Mortgage Plans

When you first begin repaying your mortgage loan, a large portion of each payment will go toward interest. This will continue for several years. As you continue to pay, however, a smaller share of each payment will be for interest, and a larger share can go toward repaying the principal, or the amount you have borrowed. The interest charges decrease as you decrease the amount owed on the principal of your loan. As the outstanding principal is reduced through your regular payments, you build equity.

When your last mortgage payment is made, all principal and interest will have been repaid. The loan will have been completely paid off.

The amount of the monthly mortgage payments for principal and interest that is settled on at the time of purchase does not change during the life of the mortgage. This makes it important that you shop around to obtain the best mortgage possible. There are a few things in any mortgage that can vary, including the interest rate, the term of the loan, and the service charge.

Checklist for Finding the Right Mortgage

Lending institution	Amount of loan you can obtain	Interest rate of loan	Amount of down payment required	Monthly payments	Method of making payments	Time you have to repay entire loan

Make sure that your mortgage contains a prepayment clause. This clause allows you to pay your mortgage in full before the due date without having to pay a penalty charge. If your mortgage does not contain this clause, you may have to pay a penalty charge for paying off the loan early. If you sell the house and use the money from the sale to pay off the mortgage, you may also be charged. It's best to consult your broker or bank to find out whether your mortgage has this important clause. Federally chartered savings and loan associations are not allowed to impose a prepayment penalty on mortgages in excess of 8 percent.

Do some intelligent comparison shopping for your mortgage. The preceding page is a checklist of items you should be noting as you check out various lending institutions and types of mortgages. See how the plan offered by each place you visit fits in with your home-buying power.

3

Where Should You Buy?

If you have decided to buy a home and have determined what you can afford, the next thing to consider is where you want to live. Before jumping in and buying your dream home in the wrong place, you must carefully go over your requirements. Otherwise you may end up in a nightmare.

You may be moving to a totally different part of the country or staying in the same general area you now live in. In either case, you probably know where you will work, but you may not have decided where you will live.

Should your new home be in a city, a town, the country, or a suburb? Your individual needs, coupled with those of your family, should dictate where you move. You must analyze those needs thoroughly in order to choose the right place. To do so, several factors need to be considered.

Distance to Place of Work

The main consideration in regard to location should be your job. Let's face it—that is what is ultimately going to pay for the home. There are only two matters of concern here:

1. How are you going to get to work?
2. How long is it going to take you to get there?

Decide the maximum amount of time you are willing to spend getting to work and consider how you are going to get there. By car? train? bus? Then buy a map of the area and calculate the time radius around where you will work—that is, figure out just where you can live to get to work in the time allowed.

If you are thinking about driving, look at the highways. Is there only one major artery going into the business area? That could mean heavy traffic at rush hours. How do you feel about that? Will a decision to drive to work mean you will have to buy a second car? There is not only the cost of the car to consider but also the expense of gasoline, insurance, and upkeep. Furthermore, check the parking facilities where you work or, if you are changing jobs, will work. Parking may also be an additional cost.

In this time of soaring gas prices, public transportation is a good alternative to driving. Look at your map again and check the railroad lines and the bus routes. If you do not have or do not want to buy a car, nearness to public transportation is crucial.

Before you start looking for a home, try out different methods of getting to work. Make the drive at 8:00 A.M. or take the train or the bus. See if the trip is acceptable to you. If not, try it from a different area within the time radius you have marked off on your map.

Consider how commuting will be during the different seasons. If you have to spend more than twenty minutes on a train, you might pick a town along a railroad line that has modernized service. That means reliable heating in the winter and air conditioning in the summer. It will make a big difference in how you feel once you get to your job or back home.

Marital Status

Marital status is the next consideration in buying a home in the right place. Are you married? single? And—very important—do you plan to remain that way? Do you have small children, grown children, or no children, and is the number likely to change?

Living in an area where you will meet people your age with similar interests should be a big consideration. This is especially true for singles. Many single people—whether bachelor, widow(er), or divorce(e)—find loneliness their greatest problem. Making friends and doing things with them is a good way to avoid being lonely.

If you are interested in meeting people through shared interests and activities, choose an area that has plenty going on nearby. University towns offer a wide variety of activities for people of all ages. Singles may find this especially attractive. Make sure the area you choose will allow you to pursue your special hobby—if you are an avid golfer, you will not be happy where you have to fight miles of rush-hour traffic to get to a fairway. Likewise, if you love to fish, desert living may not be for you!

Mobility is another consideration, again, possibly more so for a single person. If you think that it's quite possible that you'll move again before too long, buy a home that will sell easily. Be extra careful not to lock yourself into a way of life that may pall after a while. If you want to get away from it all by trying out a new life-style—buying a cabin in the woods, for example—beware. Better rent for a year and then decide.

Children

Couples with children have an entirely different set of requirements. For those without children, the quality and location of local schools may be of little importance. For young marrieds considering having children, such concerns may be crucial.

It is not enough to have a real estate broker tell you that the local schools are terrific. Remember, the broker wants to sell you on the town as well as on the house. Chances are he or she does not handle houses five miles away, where there may be better schools.

Go to see the schools yourself. If your children are in elementary school, look also at the middle and high schools. You would not want to have to move when the oldest child finishes sixth grade. Talk with the principal and some of the teachers. Ask the size of classes, what is being taught, the educational goals of the district, the number of high school graduates entering college, and the types of schools recent graduates have been attending. Talk to the athletic coach; find out about after-school programs.

Your property taxes help pay for schools. If education is important to you but finances are difficult, look for a modest home in an area of high property values. Such homes are there.

Your Age

You and your spouse may be parents of grown children who do not live with you. If so, most likely you have more money to spend than you used to and more time to enjoy leisure activities. Therefore, if you are moving to a new area, such things as restaurants, shops, golf courses, and tennis courts may loom larger in your list of concerns than they used to. By all means, take these things into consideration before you select where you are going to live. You certainly do not need to live in a community with outstanding schools. Remember, property taxes pay for these, and why add to your expenses if you are not benefiting from these taxes?

If you are over sixty, think realistically about the type of housing you choose. The work of the physical maintenance of a house could be hard to do yourself. In such cases, a condominium or a cooperative might be a good idea. If you think you may want to move again, choose a home that will sell easily in an area that is not likely to decline.

If you are an older person and want to own your own home, it's wise to pick a place to live where your costs will remain as fixed as possible. Social Security and job pensions do not keep up with inflation. A neighborhood with high property taxes to support nearby schools will be a drain on your hard-earned savings.

Heating prices are a major force in pushing up the cost of living. If you are moving to a new area, try to choose one in which your heating and air-conditioning bills will be minimal. Florida, for instance, is great on heating but a disaster for cooling.

There are two things older people should not compromise on:

1. A town or city with good medical facilities.
2. A town or city with good public transportation. You must be able to get to the grocery store fifteen years from now.

And finally, a word of caution. You may think it would be nice to move where your children live and help with the grandchildren. This is something to discuss very honestly with your children before committing yourself to a move. If they are against it, do not feel hurt. In the long run, if you consider their wishes, it will mean happy times for years to come. Furthermore, your grandchildren may really be too much for you, and you may be taking on obligations you don't really want.

Community Services

Another factor in selecting an area in which to buy your home is what the town or city will offer you. Most of the things a town or city provides come from taxes its residents pay. It is a simple matter to get a copy of the town or city budget from the borough hall, city hall, or comparable office. Many real estate brokers also have them on hand.

The basic things you should be concerned with are services and recreational facilities. Discuss each category with people who know the area.

Garbage pickup. At first glance, this may seem like a very small matter, but life is made up of a lot of such trivialities. Efficient garbage removal should have a high priority in your judgment of an area. Garbage should be picked up at least twice a week. It is better if it is removed from the rear yard, rather than from the street in front of the house. Setting garbage out in the street is a heavy chore and one that is easy to forget about.

Leaf removal. Find out if the town or city has leaf removal. Otherwise it may be difficult to get rid of thirty-five bags of leaves every fall.

Snow removal. Make sure streets and sidewalks are cleared promptly and safely. You will have to do your own walk and driveway—a fact not to be overlooked in deciding how far off the road you want your house to be.

Sewage system. Life will be simpler if your home is on the main sewage line rather than having its own cesspool or septic tank. Some areas do not have adequate sewage facilities—look into this situation before you buy.

Police and fire departments. Let us hope that you never need these services; but in case you do, make sure they are adequate. Some areas have only volunteer fire departments, and if you are putting a lot of money in your home, having to rely on volunteers may not be particularly reassuring.

In addition to the above services, your taxes will also go for recreational facilities—the maintenance of parks, swimming pools, public tennis courts, and a library. If these facilities are important to you, visit them. See what you are getting for your money.

Specific Neighborhoods

Once you've decided on a community, you should find a suitable location for yourself within that community. A close examination of neighborhoods will have to await your visits to individual homes, but you can make some preliminary judgments just by looking at a map. Check potential locations for the following:

Distance to public transportation. How will you and your spouse get to work? to the doctor's office? to the library? For decades the answer for millions of Americans has been the automobile. You might consider (or have to consider) living within walking distance of public transportation to avoid traffic jams and heavy gasoline bills.

Distance to shopping areas. It is very nice to be able to walk where you need to go. Many people often do not get enough exercise, and it would be beneficial to live within walking distance of shops, movies, restaurants, and the like.

Distance to schools. It will simplify everybody's life if your children can walk to school or the school arranges for bus transportation.

Distance to play areas. Also think about where your children are going to play. Are there other children in the neighborhood? Is there a park? a school field or playground? Are the yards situated on busy streets? How far will you have to drive the children to play areas? Do you want to do that driving?

Stability of area. Is there a likelihood that the neighborhood will go downhill? Since you must protect your investment, consider only property that will appreciate in value.

Obviously, there are no hard and fast rules for deciding where to locate. To a large extent, your decision will be made for you by the demands of your job, the availability of housing, the limitations of your bank account, and so forth. But make use of what flexibility you do have. In a way, when you buy a home, you are also buying a place in the community. Be sure the community of your choice will serve you well.

4

How Should You Look
For a House?

Now that you've examined your finances and explored different neighborhoods, you're ready to find and buy your home.

How you conduct your house-hunting expeditions can have a great deal to do with your future satisfaction with your home. You should not make haphazard investigations of homes but should look at them with an awareness of construction pluses and pitfalls.

Look Before You Buy

The first priority in house hunting is thoroughness. Look and ask around before you buy. Nothing is more foolish or costly than buying a home on impulse. And nothing may be more frustrating than finding your dream home *after* you've bought another.

So, open up all your channels of information. Let your family, friends, and neighbors—even your coworkers—know you're in the market. Often you can profit from the hard-won experience of someone who has already bought a home. Friends may know of homes for sale in their own neighborhoods or be able to direct you to a reliable real estate agent.

Look at the real estate section in newspapers. You may be attracted to the type of home you hadn't even thought of before. And you'll get an idea of price ranges in different neighborhoods.

If you're considering a move to a different city or town, read the local papers for that area. You'll get a good feel for the area and the housing market.

Ask real estate agents about the ins and outs of house hunting. Find out whether what you want in a home is currently on the market.

Finally, do some intelligent scouting on your own. A wide exposure to different homes for sale will make your final decision far more rewarding.

It's a good idea to keep a house-hunting notebook. This should contain clippings of real estate ads and your notes on the following features of each home you may be considering.

- price
- name of the owner
- location
- number of bedrooms and baths
- heating costs
- special features

This notebook can be invaluable to you. It will jog your memory of the details of certain homes you've seen. It will also allow you to compare the merits of all the homes you're considering.

Buying Directly from the Owner

Most homes are sold either through real estate advertising or through real estate agents and brokers. In some cases, however, homes can be bought directly from the owner.

It is fine to buy directly from the owner if you've looked at enough homes and neighborhoods to feel comfortable with your decision. If you buy directly, be prepared to learn all phases of the home-buying process on your own. You should keep in close contact with an attorney schooled in such matters. As in buying any home, it would be wise to get the home you are considering appraised independently. Become as well informed beforehand as you can when you buy directly or you may learn about home construction and repair the hard way.

Working Through Professionals

The more usual route to home ownership is to use the services of a real estate broker, agent, or salesperson. These people are licensed professionals. Their job is to bring home sellers and home buyers together.

Brokers or agents get paid only when the sale is completed, so it is in their best interest to arrange the best possible deal for both parties. The seller, not the buyer, pays the broker the real estate commission, which is usually 6 to 7 percent of the purchase price. Remember, however, that the broker is primarily working for the seller of the home. So use all your knowledge about homes to judge whether or not a real estate deal suits you.

ADVANTAGES OF USING A BROKER

Real estate professionals have considerable knowledge of market values, what homes are available in your price range, and what homes will fit your needs, as well as detailed information about individual homes. Your broker can tell you about mortgages, applications, and property taxes as well as about schools, churches or synagogues, and services in the neighborhood. He or she can lead you to real estate appraisers, licensed engineers, and specialists in various building trades. Brokers can help in all stages of the home-buying process. They can give you information you might otherwise never come across. When you work through a broker, you have direct access to a vast store of information and expertise.

FINDING A GOOD BROKER

There are various groups of real estate professionals.

1. A Realtor is a broker who is highly qualified, having satisfied certain standards beyond state licensing requirements. About 500,000 real estate brokers belong to the National Association of Realtors. They are pledged to the Realtor's Code of Ethics, which calls for a certain standard of performance.

2. A Realtist is another highly qualified professional, who belongs to the National Association of Real Estate Brokers.

3. A real estate salesperson is sometimes employed by builders or developers. However, the developer does not have to employ fully licensed people. Only when functioning in a brokerage capacity is a real estate broker or agent legally required to be licensed. ·

You can often find a good broker by asking family and friends whom they would recommend. You can also consult the mortgage officers in local banks.

When reading the real estate section of the news-paper, pay attention to which brokers advertise houses in neighborhoods you're interested in.

All authorized brokers must have their licenses displayed in their offices. You can check the qualifications of real estate agents and find out what properties and areas they specialize in by asking the chamber of commerce, the local real estate board, and the Better Business Bureau for lists of Realtors, brokers, and salespersons.

MEETING WITH YOUR BROKER

Your best bet for finding and financing the right home is to give your real estate broker as much information as possible. Your broker needs to know how much you can afford and what types of homes and neighborhoods you prefer.

Be straightforward with your broker. When you discuss financing, give him or her an honest estimate of

- how much you earn now
- what you expect to earn
- what your home-buying power is
- what you wish to spend on a home

Don't misrepresent your financial status. The broker needs and expects you to be truthful; there's no point in looking for a house that you can't afford.

Tell your broker as much as you can about the house you have in mind.

- What style of architecture do you especially like?
- How large a home do you need—how many bedrooms, how many baths, and so forth?
- How much land do you want to own? Is a

large backyard or a swimming pool important to you and your family?
- What special features are you looking for in a
home?
- What kind of neighborhood is best for you
and your family?

Be sure also to mention things you *don't* want in a
home or neighborhood. If you can't stand living on or
near a busy street, across from an apartment
complex, or in view of a shopping center, say so at the
beginning.

The better the picture your broker can form of
you and your needs, the faster he or she can bring you
and your home together.

Your relationship with your broker is a two-way
one. You should never hesitate to ask questions or to
have your broker explain a term or plan you might be
unfamiliar with. Don't hesitate to ask your broker to
let you see a home that interests you a number of
times to be sure you want to buy it. The real estate
professional is there to make your house hunting as
painless and informed as possible.

FINDING A HOME THROUGH YOUR BROKER

When you first meet with your broker, it will be
an armchair house hunt—you won't leave the broker's office. The broker will acquaint you with the
area you're interested in. If you are new in the area,
he or she will first give you information concerning
the town or city where you're looking for a home.
You'll get information on the town's population, what
property taxes are like in the area, and whether there
have been or will be major area changes or improvements. Your broker will also let you know what

schools, churches or synagogues, hospitals, and service centers are located in the area. Ask the broker for a map of the town you're looking over. This should come in handy when you are considering how a particular house fits into the general scheme of things.

Next, the broker will probably show you pictures of homes available in your price range. You'll want to get more specific answers to the following questions.

- How close are major transportation routes?
- What kind of schooling is available?
- How close is this home to hospitals and recreational and shopping facilities?
- What particular churches or synagogues are near these homes?

Don't be discouraged if the asking price of a home is higher than the amount you're able to spend. Home buying is sometimes a matter of bargaining; the owner may be willing to lower his or her price. Also, homes may have higher asking prices in top home-buying seasons, such as early spring. The price may come down once the peak season is over. The length of time a home has been on the market can also influence its price. Bear all this in mind when you discuss purchase price. Compare and contrast the prices of similar homes. You can also arrange for an independent appraisal by a company not involved in the sale.

When you examine pictures of houses on the market, remember that the pictures may not do the home justice. A house itself may look far more attractive in summer than in stark winter light. Camera angles can also influence a home's appearance. So don't rule out a home by the way it looks in a real estate picture. If the description of the home otherwise intrigues you, by all means put it on your list of those to see.

After you've decided which homes appeal to you, your broker will begin taking you around to see them. While this step is a preliminary to the intensive inspection you'll give homes that really interest you, it's very important to look carefully at each house you see.

Bring with you your house-hunting notebook. Jot down your impressions of view, layout, and style of each home. Also note your broker's descriptions of each property. Always listen carefully. If the home's owners are describing some features of the home, pay attention to whether they seem to be giving accurate descriptions or glossing over problem areas. People often drop more information than they realize, so make note of any suspected problems or defects.

Also bring your map of the town or city where the home is located. Mark the position of the home on the map. Later you'll be able to figure out how close the home is to transportation, schools, hospitals, churches, or synagogues.

You might find it helpful to bring a tape measure to measure windows, wall space, and so on. You may want to jot down the exact dimensions of a room for later comparisons.

Before you go into a house, ask your broker these questions:

- What is the asking price for this home?
- How long has it been on the market?
- Why are the current owners selling it?

Be sure to enter your broker's answers to the questions in your notebook. Facts on hand can save a lot of time and guesswork later on.

Pay special attention to the reasons given by the present owners for selling. Moving to another town because of business is one thing. But if the owners are, for example, "moving down the street to a smaller home," this may be a clue that something is wrong. Either the house is too big for the family, *or* the heating and maintenance bills are astronomical. Check further before you commit yourself.

After you've seen the house, you may want to ask your broker what the lowest price he or she thinks the home's seller will settle for. The most probable answer will be the list price. Remember, the broker is representing the seller. Only if directed by the seller can the broker state a lower price.

Be prepared to go on many such house-inspection trips with the same broker. You need to become as familiar as possible with many aspects of house construction before you can make an informed decision. Don't feel that you're being a pest; remember that the broker works on commission. It's in his or her best interest, as well as yours, to find you the right home in the right neighborhood at the right price.

5

How Should You Look at the Outside of a House?

Many Realtors begin the tour of a house with the interior. Before you enter the home you are looking at to see what it would be like to live inside it, however, you may wish to check out the condition of the outside of the house. And before you even look at the actual structure of the home, you must take into consideration the grounds and the surrounding neighborhood.

The Site

When you look at the outside of a home, first consider the site, the place where the home stands. How well is the property landscaped? Are there any sheds, fences, or other structures on the property? Could certain features of the property cause problems later on?

TREES, SHRUBBERY, FLOWERS

A home surrounded by tall and beautiful shade trees is highly desirable. Trees are pleasant to look at and provide shade during long, hot summers. There are also some practical advantages to having them on the site. Trees add to the value of the house, a fact to be considered if you are thinking of reselling at some time in the future. Even a property with just a few young trees may one day have some fine oaks and elms that will increase the money value of the home. The shade provided by trees also serves a practical purpose. By protecting your house somewhat from the sun's heat, trees can significantly lessen your air-conditioning needs. Just as important, trees can help provide that extra bit of privacy that is so valued a part of home ownership in the first place.

You must, however, realize that trees can be troublesome. Check to see if there are any dead or dying trees—dead limbs may eventually cause damage, and the costs of tree surgery and tree removal are high. Remember, too, that young pine or birch growing right next to the front walk might well require constant trimming, or even downright removal, before too long. Tree roots growing under sidewalks can raise the cement, creating hazardous conditions. You are responsible for the upkeep of the sidewalks bordering your house.

Bushes are another natural feature that adds value to a property. In many ways they may be less bothersome than trees. Maintenance is generally easy and inexpensive (unless you want to keep them carefully manicured—and that's entirely up to you), and they make convenient, attractive substitutes for fences or other structures that need constant upkeep. If the lot looks bare and needs shrubbery, you may well find yourself with this extra cost in time and money.

Flower gardens are the crowning glories of many homes. If the home you look at has a great deal of space set apart for gardening, and you want to be the pride of the local garden club, all is well. If you aren't an amateur gardener (and don't know whether you want to be one), you should consider the possible disadvantages. Maintaining a flower garden is time-consuming and sometimes hard work. You really have to be willing to treat your flowers with tender, loving—and constant—care. All true gardeners will fill you in on the joys of raising flowers; however, if you don't want those joys for yourself and don't want to hire a gardener, think twice before investing in a home with extensive gardening space.

You may want to have an old garden plot sodded over, but that can be an expensive project. Even then, newly sodded ground itself requires a fair amount of care until it finally becomes a part of your lawn. Before you make any decision, however, remember that a handsome bed of flowers may raise the price of a home in the springtime—something to consider when you're buying a house or selling one.

SLOPE OF THE LAND

The slope of the land on which the home stands is particularly important. See whether or not the home is below street level. If it is, you may be in for some headaches. You may find that rainy weather brings with it a basement full of water. This, in turn, can weaken the foundation of the house and lead to costly repairs. Insects like to occupy damp areas close to the ground; they may feel more at home in your low-lying house than you do.

If your prospective home is considerably higher

than street level, you may have difficulties of a different sort. Check out the driveway. Is it especially steep? curved? narrow? If so, it may be dangerous. Imagine your car parked on such a driveway in the middle of winter. A moment with your foot off the brake or a faulty emergency brake could result in serious injury or property damage.

In either case—whether the home stands below street level or above—maintenance will probably turn out to be a special problem. You don't have to be old and tottering to get tired while moving uphill. And shoveling walks or raking leaves is particularly hazardous when you have to work against a slope. Think of the potential dangers and discomforts involved in that beautifully landscaped lot. What now seems pretty enough may turn out to be a pain in the neck.

ORIENTATION OF THE HOUSE

One important element in home buying is often overlooked because it does not involve the physical condition of the structure itself or the grounds. That is the orientation of the house—how it is situated in relation to the points of a compass (north, south, east, west). Consider where the sun will strike. Sunlight will affect your home and you in several ways. A building that gets plenty of sun will probably have lower electricity bills. In addition, the play of light and shade on your home will add to its beauty as well as its comfort. And a lawn that gets plenty of sunlight is likely to stay green and healthy. Houseplants, too, will grow well with good amounts of sunlight.

If you are considering a home that faces north, you should be aware that less direct sunlight will fill your living area. The front walk and front steps will get icier in wintertime. And, in general, you will have to spend more time and effort maintaining the approaches to the house. (Wet leaves settled in a corner and out of sunlight tend to stay wet. Under the sun's rays, they will dry quickly and be much easier to remove.)

Finally, try to determine how the home stands in relation to wind currents. The direction and intensity of winds will depend as much on local factors as on large-scale weather patterns, so check with the local weather bureau to find out the way the wind blows in your particular region. Will the front door open into a dry and dusty west wind? When you open the dining room window on a warm summer evening, will you get a refreshing breeze or a tropical blast? When you're buying a home, such things count.

ACCESS WAYS

The access ways to the house should also be examined. The walks can be purely functional or can add considerably to the beauty and style of your home. Cement walks are the most common and the least troublesome. Little maintenance is required. They may, of course, crack in the course of a spring thaw or chip when your child goes roller skating, but such things can happen on any kind of surface. Cement walks are also safest. They are unlikely to produce jagged edges. In addition, they have enough roughness to provide secure footing—when not covered with ice, that is.

Brick walks are more difficult to maintain. The cracks between bricks may catch more than their share of the neighborhood dirt and may be difficult to clean out. And no matter how careful you are, *some* bricks will eventually work loose, which can create a potentially hazardous situation. Nonetheless, brick walks are generally pretty safe. They provide good traction and are comfortable surfaces for walking, skipping, and running.

A flagstone pavement is perhaps the most attractive. However, there are certain disadvantages to such a walk. Considerable maintenance is needed. Flagstones, by and large, chip far more readily than either cement or brick. In addition, it is easy for weeds to wedge their way through the cracks; you can expect to see clumps of greenery if the walk has not been attended to for even a short period of time. Slipperiness is the other possible problem. The smoother the stone, the greater the likelihood of painful falls and high hospital costs.

If the home you are looking at has no walks at all, there will be more problems. A well-beaten path to the front door is fine for a cabin at a lake, but in rainy weather it brings plenty of tracked-in mud into a home. You will probably want to have a walk put in sometime later, so now might be a good time to check into the costs of laying a walkway.

The other major access way to a home is the driveway. Here you must be especially choosy and on the lookout for possible dangers and difficulties. The children's play area should be a comfortable distance away—if given half a chance, a young child will find the driveway an ideal place for playing games, and the rearview mirror of a car is not a sufficient safeguard.

A paved driveway is the best. A gravel driveway serves the purpose, but gravel is not as good as pavement on almost all counts. The surface can become uneven and possibly dangerous. The gravel itself may scatter, leaving open areas where the ground becomes muddy and slippery. Weeds, the homeowner's nightmare, can make your driveway unsightly and bumpy. And, as with an unpaved walk, a gravel driveway may someday require paving—at your expense.

One more word on access ways: A house that is right on the street will be open to noise and possibly to car exhaust. If you have the choice, it might be better to have a longer driveway that takes a bit more time to shovel in the winter than a small patch of pavement that brings the street noise right into your living room.

NEIGHBORHOOD

When looking around the site, note the state of the neighboring houses. What condition are they in? Are they falling apart? old and elegant but in need of a paint job? small but well kept? This should tell much about the quality of life in the neighborhood. You can see if the neighborhood is growing, vital (perhaps *too* vital—that is, on its way to overcrowding and congestion), or headed for a gradual decline. This has particular importance in terms of resale value. A decaying neighborhood might seem to offer some good bargains now, but will *you* have to give a buyer an even better bargain if you decide to sell in a few years? Incidentally, if you don't feel that the asking price of the house reflects the condition of homes around it, you might be able to convince the seller to adjust the price.

A look around might also give some indication of local zoning practices. You will be able to tell if the district is highly commercial (and likely to get more so) or strictly residential. In some cases, there will be cluster zoning—residential areas carefully isolated from small, convenient business areas. Here the main consideration is simply whatever suits you. A house sandwiched between Burger City and Lou's All-Nite Bowl may fulfill all your childhood dreams, or it may drive you up the wall. Follow your tastes.

At the same time, think of what local zoning laws may mean for the future. If you are considering enlarging your home or extending your property, zoning ordinances may get in the way. Or the neighborhood that is now a paradise of open space and gentle breezes may soon be a superhighway. Zoning *will* affect you, possibly for the good. A home located in a carefully zoned area will probably retain its property value. For detailed information about zoning practices and regulations, check with your local authorities.

You might want to get some idea of what the neighbors are like. Don't hesitate to simply stop a few people and ask them appropriate questions. In most cases, they'll be more than happy to oblige with straight answers. (You may find out more than you want to know!)

By this time, you will have very thoroughly checked out the condition of the lot on which the home you are considering stands. You can use the checklist on the next page to determine whether the physical setting is right for you.

Outside Structure and Condition of House

Now we come to the house itself. The condition of the exterior, or outside, can tell you a great deal

Checklist for Site

	CONDITION			MAINTENANCE REQUIREMENTS
	Good	Fair	Poor	
Trees				
Bushes				
Flowers				
Slope of land				
Orientation of House Walks (Check one.) cement ⎯⎯ brick ⎯⎯ flagstone ⎯⎯ other ⎯⎯				
Driveway				
Neighborhood				

about the general quality of the dwelling. In addition, you want to figure out what it will take—in dollars as well as in time spent—to keep your house in good condition. How you feel about your home depends a lot on the condition of the home on the outside, so it's worth a thorough going-over.

WALLS

The sides, or outside walls, are the most visible parts of the exterior of a house, so look them over carefully. A wall surfaced with plain shingles has some strong points. Shingles can last a lifetime, though they will turn brittle with age. The unpainted varieties are far and away the easiest on upkeep. Depending on the materials of which they are made, shingles will usually prove easy to clean. A mild detergent solution should be enough to remove the stains and dirt that build up over the years. However, the weathered look can be attractive. Shingles have the further advantage of being replaced easily and cheaply. A tear or hole in one shingle need not require the taking apart of a whole section of wall; a part of an afternoon and a touch of fix-it skill are all that is needed.

Aluminum siding has similar advantages. Very little upkeep is required. A good washing once a year will keep your home bright and beautiful. Colors will not fade quickly or chip on aluminum. Durability is long. As with a shingled surface, the siding should last for an average life span. More so than either wood or many synthetics, aluminum will stand up under the ravages of the weather.

However, replacement costs can be considerable. Aluminum, after all, can be damaged or bent, and telltale scratches are not always easy to hide. If you live in an area where there is much hail, aluminum siding may not be the best idea.

Brick is the sturdiest building material for your outside walls. Barring major catastrophes, it will last forever. Naturally, a brick surface will not be perfect. Individual bricks may chip or crack, and not all bricks will be the same in size or in texture. Cleaning may be a bit of a problem. On glazed brickwork, a light scrubbing with soap and water should be sufficient. For more porous surfaces, you will probably have to hire a professional cleaner who has the right equipment and the know-how to do the job.

The only real maintenance headaches with a brick structure have to do with the mortar that holds the bricks together. This can dry, crack, and crumble through the combined effect of wind, rain, freak accidents, stresses and strains in the walls, and so on. Repair costs can be high. If you fail to replace worn or crumbling mortar, you may be in for unexpected additional expenses. Leaks may begin to appear inside the house, weakening the wall structure and causing damage to your nicely finished interior. Windows may become loose—a hazardous and annoying situation. Find out if the building has recently been tuck-pointed. This means that the mortar joints between the bricks have been reinforced with putty or fine lime mortar.

What are the warning signs of mortar wear? The walls are not as solid as they should be if the spaces between the bricks seem of uneven depth, if the mortar is dry and dusty, if you notice slipshod patching jobs, or if there are cracks running alongside certain bricks and extending upward and sideways.

Perhaps the most common form of siding, at

least in older homes, is wood. Certainly a wood surface can be pleasing to the eye. This, however, is a matter of personal taste.

A wood exterior does have some practical advantages. Unpainted wood is resistant to wear and tear and will weather very slowly. Painted wood is also weather-resistant, but you will have to devote some attention to it periodically in order to maintain it. It will have to be repainted from time to time, though not too often; once every four to six years should be sufficient. The costs of repainting are considerable, so give this some thought before you buy. Bear in mind that the quality of paints will differ. A cheap brand on the home you're looking at may have to be painted over before too long. If you choose to have the outside redone, you probably should spend the few extra dollars it takes to get an attractive, durable house paint.

Of course, there are other kinds of wall material available on the market today. A stucco surface can be very attractive, but it will require some looking after. Stucco can crack and peel and might need fairly frequent repainting. Stone, depending on the type, has many of the advantages of brick but can be expensive and difficult to repair.

TRIM

Look at the framework that surrounds the doors and windows of the house. Is it clean and newly painted? faded? cracked? uneven or sometimes out of line with the rest of the house?

Notice the quality of the paint job. If the paint is peeling or cracked, you will have to think in terms of repainting. It might also indicate that the material underneath (especially if it's wood) may not be in very good condition. You obviously do not want trim work that is rotting or decaying.

ROOF

The appearance of the roof over your head is perhaps less important than its practicality. The main concern is whether it will provide adequate protection. However, you should consider looks as well as strength. A flat roof will not add to the beauty of your home, but it is the most accessible (for doing repairs, setting up the TV antenna, or sweeping off debris) and, if well sealed, will resist leakage. A pitched roof can take many forms—a single slope, an inverted V, a hipped roof (which is sloped on both ends as well as front and back), a gabled (ridged) roof, or variations on any of these—all of them offering roughly the same advantages and disadvantages. Water runoff will be assured with any of these types of roof, but they can be more difficult to climb up on.

How can you determine the condition of the roof? Look along the outer edges. Are the shingles curled or drooping? Do they have rips or chinks? If so, you can safely assume that the roof is comparatively old and has not been kept up well. Poor repair work indicates a patch job and means that the roof is already into its declining years. Since damage by unusual and unpreventable accidents, such as storm damage, is generally covered by insurance, there is no good excuse for a roof with haphazard and amateurish repair work.

Look also for missing shingles. If you can't get a good look at the entire roof, you might try a walk through the attic to locate discolorations and possible leaks. It's in your interest to see to it that nothing is overlooked.

Remember that the greatest roof damage tends to occur in the valleys—those points on the roof where two slopes meet to form a V. Open valleys are those in which the shingles are joined by some kind of waterproof material. Woven valleys, on the other hand, have two sides that meet without a break. The latter may be less apt to develop leaks, but neither type is foolproof.

Each of the various kinds of material used in roofing has its own special qualities. A slate or tile roof is long-lasting and tough. Many people find such roofs extremely attractive, especially if the home is of a Spanish ranch-style design. However, slate and tile are brittle as well as hard and can break. Repair costs can be high. In addition, they are not easy surfaces to work on; a bit of rain will make them slippery and therefore dangerous. Asbestos-cement surfaces have roughly the same characteristics.

Asphalt shingles are favorites among home builders and most homeowners. They are relatively cheap and durable (the good ones will last fifteen years) and easy to replace. Their flexibility allows them to bend a little with the stresses and strains of an ordinary rooftop. Be sure the shingles on your home are of good quality; some cheap brands are on the market and do not provide sufficient protection for the home. Wood shingles, of course, are also available. They can be durable and strikingly beautiful, but they are fire hazards. Metal (for example, aluminum or tin) roofs are rarely appropriate to a home—they sound like kettledrums in a rainstorm, and they sizzle in the sun.

The part of your roof that can cause the most

trouble is also the least obvious to the eye. The gutters, which run the length of the roof edge to carry away the water runoff, can be easily ignored when they're working properly. But when they get clogged or broken, you'll find the rain that falls onto the front steps and into the front yard most annoying. Examine the gutters for leaks, cracks, and weak spots. If the downspouts are too narrow or have a number of twists and turns, leaves and mud may easily collect and cause hard-to-remove stoppages.

The material from which the gutters are made should be noted. Vinyl gutters do not require painting. Aluminum ones may be given a coat of paint if you choose, but this is purely optional. However, if the home you're considering has gutters made of some other metal, you should figure on a new coat of rustproof paint every few years.

ENTRANCEWAYS

If this particular home has a porch, you should give it at least a quick inspection. Notice the angle of the porch to the ground. Does it have a slant? If so, it may mean that the house is settling. It may also mean that the porch is poorly built. A slight tilt downward toward the outer edge is acceptable, to help in sweeping or in rain runoff. But beware of a porch that slants inward—you don't want water runoff to damage the interior of the house.

Look for telltale signs of decay. A rotting floorboard could indicate that other, stronger-looking boards are none too safe. On cement porches or stone patios, check for cracks and bulges. If the porch is enclosed, look closely at the screen frames or pillars. Are they sturdy? securely fastened? Or might they be dislodged by a stumble or an accidental fall? The screens or glass that surrounds the porch should be in good condition. A screen with tears in the middle or openings along the edges will have to be replaced. Just a few holes can make a whole screen useless; insects can be models of cleverness when it comes to finding and entering forbidden places!

If a porch is important to you, you'll want to consider its layout. Is it large enough? too large? Will you actually use it or just let it become a catchall for overflow furniture? On many older homes you'll find spacious L-shaped porches extending around the corner of the house—perfect for long, lazy summer visiting but perhaps not too practical for the busy executive or for persons who cherish their privacy.

The home you are seeing may have a simple entranceway rather than a large porch. Most of the same considerations apply. Check the entranceway for angle to the ground, signs of decay or excessive wear, general solidity, and strength. Be especially careful about the steps leading up to the door. These receive a harder beating than almost any other part of the house, and they often show it. Wood stairs are apt to break or rot or become rickety. Someone good at do-it-yourself projects can replace steps without too much trouble, but for a really handsome and lasting entranceway, you may have to hire a professional.

CHIMNEY

Before you wind up your examination of the exterior of the home, cast a glance up to the chimney. Do you see any loose bricks or cracks? Is anything off balance or slightly out of place? If you notice any-

Checklist for
Outside of the House

	CONDITION			MAINTENANCE REQUIREMENTS
	Good	Fair	Poor	
Walls (Check one.) shingles ___ aluminum siding ___ brick ___ wood ___ stucco ___ stone ___ other ___				
Trim				
Roof (Check one.) slate ___ tile ___ asbestos ___ asphalt ___ other ___				
Gutters				
Porch and entranceway				
Chimney				

thing that looks suspiciously out of kilter from so far away, chances are that up close even more serious faults will reveal themselves. Ask about it, or, better yet, have someone go up to give the chimney a thorough inspection. Better now than later.

Use the checklist on the preceding page for your examination of the outside of the home.

At last you are ready to enter the home and look at the interior. If you have been extremely thorough in your examination of the site and the outside of the building, you have already developed an eye for structural weaknesses and potential problems. You'll need to devote the same kind of careful attention to the inside, where an even larger number of things await your inspection. But take heart! If the home has so far passed most of the tests, it's likely that the interior will prove equally inviting.

6

How Should You Look at the Things You Can't See?

Some parts of your home are, for all practical purposes, invisible. The heating, insulation, air conditioning, and plumbing systems are mostly located within the walls or under the floors. Therefore, evaluation of them becomes difficult for the careful home buyer. Because these things are hidden, they are often overlooked. And, in fact, there is no way to be positive that some of the wiring isn't frayed or that a certain pipe isn't ready to spring a leak. Still, you can make some judgments concerning how well these systems work and some educated guesses about how long they will last. If, after going through the steps suggested here, you still have doubts, you should hire a professional to make a complete inspection.

Heating

Heating methods vary, and no single method is ideal. In these energy-conscious days, you must think about the high price of heating as well as the availability of certain fuels in your area. No one knows what the immediate future holds. Oil prices are steadily rising, and gas prices will probably rise as well before too long. Alternative sources of energy may soon become feasible for home heating systems. Solar heating is already being installed in many new homes. Coal, a traditional fuel that has lost favor over the years, might be reintroduced through newer, cleaner, and more up-to-date heating systems.

For the present, however, two kinds of fuel supply the power for most furnaces—oil and gas. Coal furnaces are relatively rare nowadays. Coal has proven to be far dirtier than either oil or gas and no more efficient or easy to use.

An oil-burning furnace is common and can be a perfectly safe and efficient way of heating your home. Check the size of the storage tank. For an average-sized home, a tank of 275 gallons is standard.

Of course, one of your chief concerns is cost. This is difficult to estimate, not only because of rising fuel prices but also because heating costs depend so much on the heating needs of your region and on your own living requirements. An oil system is more expensive to install than a gas system, but if you keep the oil system clean and well maintained, the difference in heating costs is (at present) small. The best way to figure your heating bill is to ask to see the previous owner's fuel bills. If an oil furnace heats the home but not the hot water, the total of the bills for oil is the total heating cost. To figure the average monthly cost, you need only divide by twelve. If the oil furnace heats both the home and the hot water, add up the fuel bills for the year and multiply by 0.8. This will give you the monthly cost of heating that home with oil. If you want to find out how many gallons of oil were used, it might also be wise to call the fuel company and ask about prices, since the actual cost of the oil per gallon may not be easy to find in the fuel bill.

You might also want to ask if the company has estimated fuel costs for the immediate future. A projection, or estimate, for the next ten years or more will help you decide whether or not oil heating is for you. If the company can't (or won't) help, there are always government agencies or offices to consult. Your local utilities office, for instance, may be able to provide information. And you can always write the Department of Housing and Urban Development office in your area to obtain their estimates of heating prices.

A gas furnace can also do a good job of providing your home with heat. Ask first about the availability of gas pipelines in the neighborhood. If there aren't many people living in the area, you may find that the expense for hooking up to the nearest gas line is high. Many homeowners who have an oil-burning furnace decide to change to gas because, while a gas setup is not necessarily cheaper than oil, it is cleaner and needs less in the way of service and maintenance. If you are thinking of doing this, you must bear in mind that this conversion process takes both time and money. The installers must add a conversion unit, replace the old oil burner with a gas burner, and get rid of the storage tank.

Once the new system is installed, however, you may decide it was worth the price. Here are some of the things to do each year to keep an oil-burning furnace properly maintained.

Clean—
burner unit
heating elements
thermostat contacts

Check—
oil leaks (if any)
electrical connections
oil pump

Adjust—
burner unit
fuel-to-air ratio
dampers
draft regulator
thermostat contacts

Change—
oil filters
air filter
burner nozzle

Compare that to the suggested checks on a gas
burner:

Clean—
thermostat contacts

Check—
main gas valve
pressure regulator
safety control valve

Adjust—
air supply nozzle
thermostat contacts

Which looks easier?
   As with an oil system, the costs of gas heat are
not easy to pin down. You should, of course, get

estimates from your local utility company based on projected prices for the next several years. And the fuel bills of the present occupant will give you a pretty good idea. You can also simply read the gas meter to determine the rate of consumption. By doing any or all of these things, you should have little excuse for blowing your top when the gas bills start coming in.

The methods by which the heat is actually carried to individual rooms will vary from home to home, but in most cases it will take some form of *dispersion*. That is, a heated substance (water or air) will be dispersed, or scattered, to different parts of the home, giving off heat as it goes.

Warm-air heating is a dispersion system widely used throughout the nation. In some of the older homes, you may see large floor registers that simply allow heat to rise into the rooms while the cold air flows downward to be reheated. Such a system takes up too much space and is not efficient. A better method is forced-air heating. Here the air is pushed by means of a blower through ducts that open into individual rooms. Since the air is distributed evenly and continuously, your home will be efficiently heated. In addition, filters can be installed to insure that debris and dirt won't clog up the works. Forced-air systems are especially common nowadays because they are cheaper to install than other systems and work at least as well.

Hot-water heating is based on a similar principle. A pump close to the furnace circulates water through a system of pipes and radiators. As the water enters the radiator in each room, the water gives off heat, cools, and is then returned to the boiler to be heated once again. Very simple and reliable. If you are sensitive to drafts, this system would be ideal for you. The best kind of hot-water boiler is cast iron and bears the seal of the Institute of Boiler and Radiator Manufacturers (IBR). A steel boiler is not as good, especially in hard-water areas, but if the home you're looking at has one, make sure it has the imprint of the Steel Boiler Institute (SBI).

Steam heat requires no circulating device at all. Water is turned to steam by the boiler and rises through the pipes and into the radiators. The steam then condenses, returning as water to the boiler to begin the cycle again. This can be an inexpensive and efficient means of heating your home. But in some cases, especially in the older systems, it can be a little noisy. Check to see if there are two pipes connected to the radiator, one leading into it and another leading away from it. If so, you have the two-pipe system—much better than the cheaper kind, which uses only a single pipe for carrying both the steam and the condensed water.

In some homes, you will find radiant hot-water heating, which simply means that water is pumped through tubes enclosed in the floor. The heat then rises into the room. Thus, you avoid rattling or ugly radiators, and you gain a nice warm floor for your barefoot midnight raids on the refrigerator.

But this form of heating does have some problems. It is both slow in delivering heat and slow in turning it down. Rugs or carpets can interfere with the heating process. Finally, if anything goes wrong, repair work is difficult and expensive; the floor has to be taken apart just to get to the source of trouble.

Something to consider in all of these systems is the type of heat outlet used. What is its condition?

Does it blend in well with the rest of the room, or is it big and ugly? Will it distribute the heat evenly?

Radiators are in widespread use around the nation, but the usual types are not very elegant additions to a room. Furthermore, they can take up much-needed wall space; you may see just the place for your TV set or sofa only to realize that the radiator would crowd it out. And you'll have to remember that the space immediately surrounding the radiator can get uncomfortably hot—too hot a place for an easy chair or a coffee table. However, this kind of outlet will heat your room efficiently.

Baseboards (found at the joint of wall and floor) can act as another outlet for heat. These have the advantage of distributing the heat evenly throughout the room and of being relatively hidden. You may have to put up with a slight bulge at the bottom edge of your walls, but this will generally not be noticeable. Of course, there is always the risk that a leak could do damage at any point along the wall, but it is a small one.

Vents provide the heat in a warm-air system. If possible, look to see if the vents in the house are clean and equipped with filtering devices. Certainly, a vent that is loose, bent, or clogged with dust should warn you that all may not be well within. Air vents should be located at or below window level.

One other method of heating deserves brief mention. Electric heat is very popular with home builders since it is easy and cheap to install. It is good for homeowners because it is clean and gets rid of the need for an involved network of pipes, radiators, furnaces, and controlling devices. If properly installed, electric heat is usually not much more expensive than either oil or gas. But if your home is not well insulated, electric heat will be very inefficient. If you are thinking of buying a home with electric heat, you should make a special point of looking into electric rates and examining the bills of the previous owner. The money you save may be your own.

Insulation

Any home without enough insulation will allow a needless waste of heat. Since fuel prices are climbing steadily and quickly, it is senseless to let heat escape through an uninsulated roof, floor, or wall.

One brief example. The Department of Housing and Urban Development (HUD) estimates that by simply insulating your attic, you can gain anywhere from $35 to $120 in yearly savings. By caulking and weather-stripping your doors and windows (two methods that seal the cracks between the frame and the window or door to prevent cold air from leaking in) you can save $30 to $75. And by using plastic storm windows on that same home, you can hold on to another $15 to $40.

In a new home, insulation may take any one of several forms. It may come in batts—that is, slabs of light fiberglass or rock wool that lie flat between attic rafters, wall studs, or floor joists (the beams supporting the floor from wall to wall). Or it may come in blankets, which are similar, except that they come in long coils that can be unrolled and fitted into place. Both kinds will resist fire and moisture.

Another form of insulation—the technical name is ureaformaldehyde—can be foamed into place. It can be used in the attic or in already finished walls, and it is an effective, though expensive, insulator. However, its overall value as an insulator remains uncertain, partly because some contractors are inexpert or careless in applying it.

Loose fill is simply insulating material in the form of loose particles. It can consist of fiberglass or rock wool, or it can be made of other synthetic materials, such as cellulosic fiber, vermiculite, or perlite. If the area to be insulated is open and accessible—an unfinished attic floor, for instance—the fill can just be poured in. Otherwise you may have to have it blown in through the use of special equipment.

No matter what kind of insulation your home has, you can determine its efficiency by using the R-Value, which is listed in the brochure that comes with the insulation you buy. The dealer you get the insulation from can also tell you its R-Value. The R-Value refers to how well your insulation will resist the flow of heat. A higher R-Value number means greater resistance and better insulation. In general, R-33 should be sufficient for the attic, R-19 for walls, and R-22 for floors. However, check with local authorities for the insulating needs and legal requirements in your area. In colder climates, higher R ratings may be called for, and builders sometimes suggest thicker insulation for homes heated by electricity.

In an older home, the state of the insulation will be a matter of special concern. Insulating methods varied widely in the good old days, and you might have to invest in some extra insulation if you want to keep your fuel bills low. In an old home that already has insulation, you should see how much there is, what kind, and where. The merits of each type have already been explained. Assuming no R-Value is given to you by the seller of the home (rating standards are a fairly recent phenomenon), you should look first for thickness. In most parts of the home, especially the attic, it is probably safe to say that insulation of less than four inches will have to be supplemented. A surer test would be to compare heating bills of the home you are interested in with those of neighboring homes. You might even ask local contractors how high fuel bills should be for a house the size of the one you are looking at. All of this takes a bit of time and trouble, but at least you'll get a reliable picture of your insulation needs.

You'll also need to find out the extent of the insulation throughout the house. Is the garage insulated and heated? Do you want it to be? Are the basement walls fully insulated? How about crawl spaces (the spaces between the ground and the floor), the air ducts, the undersides of the floors, and the attic? Remember that a properly insulated two-story house will hold heat much better than a simple single-level dwelling.

Even if the home seems thoroughly insulated, you may have overlooked a main escape route for warm air—the windows. Glass is not a very good insulator, and the ordinary single-pane kind is a notorious heat waster. The best protection is storm windows and doors, which can be single pane, though double- or triple-track aluminum window-screen combinations are preferable.

Above all, see to it that door and window frames are caulked and weather-stripped. Caulking is a puttylike substance that seals cracks between the siding and the frame. The strips of metal, rubber, or vinyl that line the inner edges of doors and windows make up the weather stripping. If either of these is broken or worn away, then cold air will seep in through the cracks.

If your home is without insulation, you may want to do the installation yourself. The batts and the blanket types are relatively easy to install. On an unfinished attic floor, you simply lay them between the joists. (Make sure the kind you buy is of the right width.) Loose fill can be poured in by hand. If ventilation is poor, you may also need to lay a "vapor barrier" (clear, heavy plastic) so that moisture won't condense and harm the new insulation. If the inside of the roof or the walls has not yet been finished with wallboard or plaster, you simply staple the insulation along the edges of the wood beams. A small flap running the length of the batt is for stapling.

To reach areas already enclosed, such as finished walls, it will probably be necessary to have the insulation blown in or foamed in. This can be expensive, but it beats trying to get along in an uninsulated home.

Air Conditioning

An air-conditioning system is a special feature in the modern home and involves special problems. Yet most people who have it would not do without it. The main reason for having air conditioning is, naturally enough, personal comfort—especially when someone is allergic to dust or pollen. There are other reasons. It combats the various harmful effects both to the home and the person of too much heat and moisture, it allows you to work more quickly and efficiently inside the home, and it keeps the home generally cleaner and safer. The drier air will be better for you and your belongings—clothes won't mildew and wood won't expand.

In many homes, the room unit is common. This is

the heavy rectangular boxlike machine that squats on the windowsill (or rests in a specially built place in the wall) and circulates cool air throughout the room. Its advantages are clear. Since it cools a limited area, you are not wasting energy on unoccupied parts of the house. In very mild or dry climates, a single machine may be all you need to keep comfortable during the summer months. Installation and repairs are relatively easy—all you need is a strong back for wrestling the thing into place.

Determining the size of the air conditioner you should buy is a tricky business. It depends on a variety of factors, including where you live, how well the home is insulated, and how much space you want cooled. Figure that every 12,000 BTUs (British Thermal Units) of air conditioning will effectively cool around 600 square feet of living area. (This number of BTUs is equivalent to a one-ton system.) For more exact figures adjusted to your specific needs, check with the air-conditioning salespeople in your area.

Central air conditioning gets more and more popular every year. If you live in a very hot climate or if the summers are extremely hot in your area, and you want to use the entire living area in comfort, a whole-house system is for you.

A forced-air heating system can be easily adapted to cooling. The air ducts will carry cool air as well as hot, so all you need is to have special air-conditioning equipment attached to the main ductwork. With a few other minor additions (and if the ducts themselves are large enough), you've got an air-conditioned home.

The advantages are self-evident. Rather than worry about keeping doors closed and huddling the family into a corner of the home, you can relax and enjoy cool air throughout. Thermostats can control the amount of cool air entering individual rooms. Your windows will not be blocked by huge cooling units. The cost of the equipment and installation will range from around $1,250 to $1,350 for a 30,000 BTU (2½-ton) system.

Other kinds of heating systems are less adaptable to central air conditioning, but good, efficient units can be installed. Costs will vary—in general, however, you can figure on paying about three or four times what you would pay for converting a forced-air system.

Wiring

The control center for the home's electrical system is the fuse box. Fuses are designed to prevent the electrical circuits from overloading. When too much current is going through a particular circuit, a small strip of metal within the fuse will melt and halt the flow of electricity (known as "blowing a fuse"). A circuit breaker does the work of a fuse but looks and operates much like a light switch. When a circuit is overloaded, the switch will simply flip to Off. Current can be restored by switching the circuit breaker back to the On position.

The main thing to look for in the fuse box is the amperage rating for the whole house. *Amperage* refers to the quantity of current that is flowing through a wire. So the amperage rating tells you the amount of electricity your circuits can carry effectively. The rating for your home is usually printed on a small plate attached to the box. A home of average size with a number of electrical appliances will require a minimum of 100-ampere service, and anything over that would be to your advantage.

Look also to see how many circuits your home is provided with. (A single-family home with moderate electricity usage will usually have from fifteen to twenty circuits.) Do this by merely counting the number of fuses or circuit breakers located in the box. Bear in mind that a heavy-duty circuit of 220 volts (a volt being the unit that measures the degree of pressure forcing the current through the wire) will probably have two circuit breakers joined together.

Outside the house, you will notice heavy wires that connect the meter box on your home to the utility pole outside. If you see three of these strong wires, you can be reasonably sure that your home is getting an adequate amount of electricity. This three-wire service is virtually a necessity in today's home. In most cases, three wires will carry a load of 220 volts, and you should check to make sure this is so.

Old homes especially may be insufficiently wired. Some are wired for as little as thirty amperes of electricity! Rewiring such a place is a project of major proportions; it is both time-consuming and expensive. A home with a two-wire, 110-volt service will be found wanting for the modern homeowner. If you use an average number of appliances in the kitchen, or if you have an air conditioner or other appliances that use a great deal of electricity, a 220-volt system should be put in. Check to see if certain of your appliances require a 220-volt service.

Problems with the wiring itself are many and varied. Aluminum is sometimes used because it is comparatively inexpensive. But it is also a poorer conductor than either copper or silver and so must make up in thickness what it lacks in efficiency. It has recently fallen out of favor because of its tendency to expand, which loosens the wiring and does harm to the outer covering. Silver wire is an excellent conductor, but it is too costly for regular household work. Copper wire is generally used. It is a fine conductor, and the price is right.

Obviously, you can't tear down all the walls to check on the condition of the wiring. But you can look around at wires that do happen to be exposed. The basement is a good place for this, especially in utility or storage rooms where the builder was less concerned with looks than with making things work. If the wires there are very frayed or cracked, the wiring probably is bad in general.

Test the light switches too. A switch that hangs loosely on the wall may indicate trouble within, or it may simply need tightening with a screwdriver. But if the lights blink or waver or just plain don't work when you flick them on, a new switch might have to be installed.

While you're at it, give the electrical outlets a quick inspection. Determine their condition and, equally important, see how many there are in each room. A common curse in older homes is that there are not enough outlets. One outlet for an entire room, even a small room, will not do. There even may be local safety regulations against it. Ideally there will be an outlet within about five or six feet of every appliance used. To make your floor a jumble of extension cords and wires all coming from one or two sockets is dangerous for several reasons. First, the exposed sections of current-carrying metal increase the chance of fire; second, you run the risk of overloading the circuits; third, the wires will be kicked about and tripped over, which does damage to the wires (to say nothing of your toes and ankles).

You do have some insurance against faulty wiring through the regulations of the National Electric Code and Underwriters' Laboratories. The national code establishes standards for electrical installation that are observed by many builders and electricians throughout the country. Underwriters' Laboratories places its stamp of approval (UL) on all electrical equipment that has been tested and found acceptable. If the electrical devices in your home bear the UL seal, then you can be sure that—barring accidents, poor installation, or the effects of too much wear—the electrical system is sound.

Plumbing

The plumbing system is another hidden part of your home. Though you can't see it, its ability to do the job of carrying in water and carrying away waste will be very important to you. Poorly made or poorly installed pipes and fixtures will give you nothing but trouble.

To determine the quality of your plumbing, check first on the condition of pipes and drains. In the basement, you will see a network of exposed pipes. Examine them for signs of past repair jobs. If what you see are patches, wires, and rags, you've got painful days ahead. Look also for signs of past flooding. The basement will often retain telltale watermarks, and you should be on the lookout for them.

The best way to test the condition of the plumbing is to turn on all the faucets in the home and flush the toilets at the same time. This will tell you if the pipes are clear of rust and corrosion. If the water flow is much reduced, some expensive replacement work may be needed.

Similarly, if the pipes make noisy, clanking sounds when you turn on the faucets, something is wrong. If you decide to buy a home with this problem, don't try to fix things yourself—consult a licensed plumber. Strongly vibrating pipes also indicate trouble and should be taken care of immediately. The vibrations will often loosen fittings and cause leaks.

There should be enough water pressure to provide a strong flow of water in two-story (even three-story) homes. If the plumbing has been properly installed, this should be no problem. But check anyway, and if the pressure seems low, call in a plumber or get in touch with your local water department.

Don't be shy about giving the toilet a thorough inspection. First, flush the toilet to see how noisy it is. A bowl with just a small pool of low-lying water will tend to be noisy and hard to clean. It is also the cheapest and should be avoided. The better bowls will hold a greater quantity of water and will flush quietly.

Finally, find out what kind of waste-disposal system you have. In highly populated areas, there will often be a public sewer system. You will have to pay to have your plumbing hooked up to the main line, but the convenience is well worth the price. Of course, things can go wrong. Sewer pipes can break or get blocked by tree roots. Still, use of the municipal disposal system is almost always a good idea for the new homeowner.

The best alternative is the septic tank. This is a large, airtight tank that converts some waste to gas and sludge and the rest to a liquid substance, which then seeps into the surrounding soil. If all goes well, a septic tank can be a perfectly good system of waste disposal. Unfortunately, things don't always go well.

Checklist for Heating, Insulation, Air Conditioning, Wiring, and Plumbing

	CONDITION			MAINTENANCE REQUIREMENTS
	Good	Fair	Poor	
Furnace (Check one.) oil ＿＿ gas ＿＿				
Heating system forced air ＿＿ hot water ＿＿ steam ＿＿ radiant hot-water ＿＿ electric ＿＿ other ＿＿				
Outlets (heating) radiator ＿＿ baseboard ＿＿ vents ＿＿ other ＿＿				
Insulation (Write in R-Value.) ceiling ＿＿ floors ＿＿ walls ＿＿ (Check one.) fiberglass ＿＿ rock wool ＿＿ foam ＿＿ loose fill ＿＿ other ＿＿				

	CONDITION			MAINTENANCE REQUIREMENTS
	Good	Fair	Poor	

Air conditioning
   room ____
   central ____				

Wiring
(Make sure there is
enough amperage.)
   copper ____
   aluminum ____
   silver ____
   other ____				

Electrical outlets (Make sure there are enough for your purposes.)				

Plumbing
   pipes
   faucets
   toilets				

Waste disposal
   public line ____
   septic tank ____
   cesspool ____				

Some types of soil will not absorb the liquid wastes well, and a breakdown can quickly turn into a health hazard. Furthermore, maintenance can be a headache. The tank will require a good cleaning every two years or so, and any kind of repair work is expensive.

Cesspools are also used for waste disposal, but they are not recommended. A cesspool, which works much like a septic tank, is less safe and is likely to clog and overflow.

If Questions Remain

This completes the painstaking and difficult business of examining the invisible parts of your home. Of course, if doubts linger, talk to a qualified professional. Your own inspection, no matter how thorough, cannot guarantee that those all-important systems between walls are in perfect shape. So get the best advice available. And then prepare yourself for a more pleasant prospect—a look at the visible features of the home's interior.

7

What Should You Look For Inside?

If the inside of your home is well designed, your life will be much simpler, and you will enjoy your home more. The problem lies in figuring out whether or not it *is* well designed. Happily, we have not yet reached the point where all interior design is the same. Homes come in all shapes and sizes, and architects like to develop new, imaginative floor plans for their clients. But this same variety makes for some confusion. What should you look for in the general layout of the home?

Entrances

We've already looked at the entranceways to the home; now it's time to consider the entrances themselves. How many are there? A large number (four or five) will make it easy and convenient to get inside. This may not be so good, though, since burglars will be as delighted by the ease as you'll be. On the other hand, a home with just one entrance is a firetrap. You'll probably want something in between. When deciding on a home, remember that a good part of moving involves simply getting the furniture from the outside of the home to the inside. Look for entrances that will allow room for you to squeeze your piano, sofa, refrigerator, or other oversized objects inside and into place.

Check the doorways for open areas and loose fittings. Here is where drafts come through and heat is lost. The doorjamb (the side of the door opening) should be tightly sealed; windows on or near the door itself should be airtight; nooks and corners should be solid and free from telltale drafts.

Notice in particular how the entrances are constructed. There should not be too much glass close by. With constant opening and closing of the doors, there is always the danger of broken glass. It is also easier for burglars to break in if there is glass in the door itself. Only very strong glass should be used in large-sized sheets around the entrance.

The position of the main entrance is very important. Is the entrance a convenient passageway to several rooms in the home? Is there an area for putting on boots, shaking off snow, or scraping mud from your shoes? Will it let in a blast of heat or cold air every time the front door opens, or will it protect you from such blasts?

The best kind of entrance is one that opens into a central hall with a large closet off to the side. This will give you an area in which to welcome guests and dispose of heavy coats, dripping umbrellas, and so on. The areaway should also be next to the living room. If your front door opens directly into the living room, all traffic will pass over your carpeting and through the carefully finished part of the home. The wear and tear will be frightful, and costs for cleaning and maintenance are likely to be high.

Some homes are built without closets near the front door. Be sure there is ample closet space somewhere not too far from the main entrance—down the hall, for example, or just off the living room.

The back entrance should open into the kitchen or a room next to the kitchen. This will make things easier for anyone cooking or doing housework. Garbage can be conveniently disposed of, and plenty of fresh air is available. A small storage area or workroom is useful for doing various household chores. If you are looking at a home whose back door opens into a plain but serviceable areaway, count it as a plus.

If a garage is attached to the house, the entrance from the garage should open into a mudroom or similar area. Once again, this will limit the effects of tracked-in mud or snow. And, again, access to a major storage area will be good.

It follows that a home with an unattached garage should have a separate back door. You do need some back entrance for safety's sake as well as convenience.

Living Room

Be sure your living room does not double as a passageway! This goes not only for its placement in relation to the front entrance but for its relation to other rooms of the home as well. If the living room is midway between the kitchen and the bathroom, expect lots of traffic.

It is a good idea to see if any bathrooms or bedrooms lie directly next to the living room. Such an arrangement will be inconvenient for several reasons. First, there are the problems mentioned before caused by heavy use. Second, the privacy you desire may be reduced. To be sure, the living room is where you entertain your guests, but you won't want your own dressing and cleaning rituals to provide the entertainment! Furthermore, you will want as much light and wall space as possible. The living room should be light and comfortable, so you'll want plenty of room for windows, couches, easy chairs, floor lamps, coffee tables, and the rest. Too many doorframes will get in the way.

In many homes, of course, bedrooms will be located in entirely separate areas of the house—upstairs, perhaps, or in the basement. If, however, there are bedrooms on the ground floor, look to see if you can go from kitchen to bedroom without passing through other rooms. The "functional" areas of the home are best kept apart from the living areas. You don't want the children underfoot when you're preparing a big meal, nor do you want to hear the blare of the TV when you're trying to get a good night's sleep.

The matter of adequate wall space should be fully considered. The problem of various rooms opening into the living room has already been mentioned. Look also for any built-in features of the room that take up valued space—for example, large picture windows, beams, radiators, or a fireplace. A built-in lamp fixture or a magazine rack may be attractive and practical, but ask yourself if such features will interfere with your furnishing plans.

The size of the living room is important. As a rule, a room that measures fourteen by twenty is thought to be a desirable size. The number of family members will determine how much space you require in the living area. If there is a special part of the home set aside for recreation or for family activities, the living room can be small and cozy. It can also be richly furnished and decorated, since the rough stuff will (with luck) take place elsewhere. If, on the other hand, the living room is the central gathering spot for you and your family, you will want plenty of space and tough, long-lasting furniture.

A fireplace may occupy a prominent position in the living room. If it is handsome and doesn't overwhelm the room, consider it an asset. Make sure it is usable if you plan to use it. But think about how it will affect your use of the whole area. If you are going to build wood fires, there should be a clearing in front of the hearth to allow the heat to spread out a little, to provide for removal of ashes, and to protect the area from flying sparks. You may want to consider whether furniture will face the fire or simply line the walls. In the former arrangement, the middle of the room will be partly blocked, and extra space will be necessary so that people can move around.

Of course, fireplaces have their problems. They can cause the home to be unevenly heated, and, since they are not the safest of your household items, care must be taken to use them correctly. The smoke in the chimney can back up into the house if the flue is accidentally shut or if the chimney is clogged. (Check how well the chimney draws by blowing some cigarette smoke into the fireplace and seeing if it rises steadily and easily.) Removing the ashes is a dirty task; also, some burn marks may appear on your carpet even if the fireplace has a properly placed protective screen in front of it.

If you think a fireplace will bring you savings, you may be right. However, your fuel costs will not necessarily be lower. In many parts of the country, firewood must be bought—and at high prices. You must be careful not to leave the flue open after the fire is out, or substantial amounts of heat will be sent right up the chimney.

Many homeowners find a fireplace highly desirable as a kind of spiritual center and source of warmth.

Dining Room

A special area for dining can take two forms—either an entirely separate room adjoining the kitchen, or an open area at one end of the living room.

If the dining room is separate, there are certain features to be considered. Are there two entrances—one coming from the kitchen and the other from the hall or a living area? The necessity of being near the kitchen is obvious, while the closeness of a hallway or living area lets your guests come to the table without passing through the kitchen.

Make sure the dining area is large enough to accommodate you, your family, and guests. You may want a large table in the center. If this is so, allow at least twenty inches of table space per person, and see how much wall space this leaves you. Of course, all a dining room really needs is a table with chairs, but some furniture along the wall will add to the comfort and attractiveness of the room. A handsome china cabinet, a buffet, or a server, for instance, would be appropriate to this part of the home.

If the dining area is an extension of the living room, many of the same considerations apply. Easy access to the kitchen is a must. There also has to be plenty of elbowroom for both family and friends. In these open dining areas, be extra careful about the problem of space. Sometimes the builder has provided a cozy-looking little nook, which looks fine at first glance but which proves to be a nuisance later on. This will be all right if you plan on doing occasional or light entertaining. Otherwise, perhaps a separate dining room would be better for your purposes.

One final tip. If people are moving out of the home you are looking at, they may have removed some of their furniture. What may look like part of a large living room when you see it bare may have been a perfectly good dining room when the dinner table was in place.

Kitchen

The kitchen is usually the working center of the home. Here is where much of the everyday business of life will be conducted. Your first and foremost concern, therefore, should be the efficiency of the kitchen area.

Check the condition of all built-in appliances. If the sink has a disposal system, give it a try. If you see a garbage compacter or a microwave oven, take time to test it.

In addition, make sure there's room for your own appliances in the new kitchen. You may have a refrigerator you want to bring with you when you move in. If there is space provided for a sixty-one-inch refrigerator and yours is sixty-four inches high, think of the remodeling and rebuilding costs that lie ahead.

Be choosy about cabinet space. This is where you'll want to keep all the essentials for cooking and, perhaps, serving—canned and packaged foods, utensils, pots and pans (the list goes on and on). That takes room and lots of it. The Federal Housing Administration (FHA) has determined that a kitchen in a four-bedroom house should have at least fifty square feet of shelf space in wall and base cabinets combined. In a three-bedroom house the minimum is forty-four square feet; in a two-bedroom house, thirty-eight square feet; and in a one-bedroom house, thirty square feet.

Counter space should be ample as well. Depending on the layout, you should have work space on at least one side of the stove, close to the refrigerator, and next to the sink. In addition, there should be some provision made for a serving area—a place to put already prepared foods until they're ready to be served. All in all, a minimum of twelve feet of counter space should be provided. With less than that, you may be cramped and uncomfortable in your kitchen.

Ask the seller if the refrigerator and stove are included. A misunderstanding here could involve expenses of hundreds of dollars. You will naturally want to know the condition of each of these appliances. If both are included, you must decide if you really want these particular models or if you'd prefer to bring in equipment that more closely matches your own needs and plans.

Ideally the stove, sink, and refrigerator should be arranged so that you can move easily from one to the other. One of these should face the other two, though this is not always possible even in carefully designed homes. In general, you should look for a kitchen in which the three form a sort of triangle; a layout like that will save many needless footsteps every day. A refrigerator that opens toward the sink will be an added convenience.

Now give the floor a quick inspection. What is it made of? Linoleum? Asphalt tile? Ceramic tile? Vinyl? Cork? Is it carpeted?

A linoleum surface is cheap and serviceable but will wear down. The cheaper brands will eventually lose their designs and will curl and crack open.

Asphalt tile is often installed in new homes, but its usefulness for the kitchen is questionable. It is not grease-resistant, it is easily cracked or dented, and wear and tear will show. Vinyl asbestos tile—a little more expensive—is preferable.

A ceramic floor is excellent for resisting buildups of grease and grime. A simple mopping or scrubbing with a detergent cleaner should be enough to keep your kitchen floor spotless. Ceramic tile is also fireproof and waterproof. But it is brittle and will break readily; in addition, the joints may discolor with age. Cork, like rubber, is springy and quiet, but it is not particularly durable. Both cork and rubber are badly affected by the buildup of oil and grease. Such floors are not really practical.

The best covering for your kitchen floor is pure vinyl. Vinyl lasts a long time. It stands up well under the continual buildup of oil and grease, and maintenance is easy. Its only drawback is expense; the cost of vinyl tile greatly exceeds that of asphalt or vinyl asbestos tile.

In recent years kitchen carpeting has become more and more popular. This kind of surface will wear very well, but make sure the carpet has been made specifically for kitchen use. It should have a synthetic foam backing with a waterproof material between the surface and the backing.

Other things to look for in the kitchen include enough space for a table for informal eating and snacking, adequate lighting (the stove, sink, and table areas should be thoroughly illuminated), and sufficient ventilation. Ventilation has special importance in the kitchen. Is there a fan above the stove? There should be one. Check the condition of the fan. Is it in good working order? Is it powerful enough to blow out smoke and hot air quickly and effectively? A ten-inch, two-speed fan will be adequate in most kitchens.

Laundry Room

Any well-designed home will have some space allotted for doing the laundry. The best arrangement is for the laundry room to be placed on the first floor near the kitchen. Thus, the washing can be conveniently done while you go about your other household chores. Unfortunately, this is not always possible. In many homes, laundry facilities will be located in the basement—a workable, if less than ideal, arrangement.

No matter where the laundry room is situated, however, there should be some provision made for storage of laundry supplies. You may have hampers, measuring cups, and boxes and bottles of detergents, softeners, and bleaches that take up shelf space and that you'll need to have handy. Make sure that at least there is room enough for some sort of cabinet you can buy yourself for storage.

Be sure to ask if the washer and dryer are included in the price of the home. If they are, give them a trial run. Washing machines are expensive. See to it that you have a serviceable one. If there is no washer or dryer, check to see what installation costs may be involved.

Bedrooms

Bedrooms are for sleeping. For this reason they should be located a respectable distance from the living areas of the home. Try to determine if the walls are thick or solid enough to muffle sounds from other rooms. A location just off the central hallway but still clearly separated from the busiest areas of the home (kitchen, living room, and dining room) is ideal.

Another consideration when looking at bedrooms is size. The adult bedroom should have space enough to hold a good-sized bed (or twin beds), dressers, and perhaps a writing desk, chairs, and a TV set. If you have a king-sized bed, you will need more space than is sometimes provided in older bedrooms. A typical king-sized bed will measure seventy-eight inches by eighty inches. You will still want open areas for dressing, laying out your clothes, and so forth.

In particular, check on closet space. Much will depend on your family's specific needs. Your wardrobe may be relatively small, though most people find that as the years go by, it's much easier to accumulate clothes than to throw or give them away. So look for large closets that are easy to get into. About six square feet of closet space per person is a bare minimum. Get more if you can.

Figure whether halls and the doorways of bedrooms are wide enough for large dressers and bed frames. When you move in or buy new furniture, the importance of this will be evident.

Bathrooms

A well-equipped home will have centrally located, carefully built bathroom facilities. Though you may have little interest in giving the bathroom a floor-to-ceiling inspection, it is worthwhile to do so. Not only is the bathroom one of the most frequently used rooms in the home, it is also one of the most dangerous. All sorts of accidents can occur here, especially to small children or to elderly persons.

A small bathroom may suit your needs. However, no bathroom should measure less than six feet by eight feet. As with most other rooms, the larger the better. More important than size is bathroom design. If fixtures are arranged for maximum safety and convenience, size won't make much difference. Some counter space on either side of the sink (with storage space beneath) is a good idea and will be included in the best bathrooms. If you think that you may want securely fastened hand bars next to the tub and toilet for safety's sake, especially for older members of your family, make sure that there is space to put them up.

How do you judge the design of the bathroom? One consideration is that if the builder has placed the window directly next to the tub or shower, there may be unhealthy drafts in the wintertime and added maintenance problems, since the moisture causes rapid deterioration of paint, wood, and putty. However, bathrooms designed this way are very common, and heavy plastic curtains can help a lot.

The floor will usually be made of some kind of resilient tile. Ceramic tile should line the walls to about chest high, which makes for easier maintenance.

The good bathtub will be made of cast iron covered by a double layer of hard, acid-resistant enamel. Cheaper varieties (the kinds you want to avoid) will have a steel base and a thin enamel covering. If you notice chips and stains on the tub, tap it to see if it has a light, metallic ring. If it does, it is probably the inferior kind. These tubs can, however, be recovered with porcelain to make a smooth surface.

Storage space in the bathroom should be ample. If there is no handy linen or supply closet, you'll need shelves for towels, shavers, soaps, shampoos, and a multitude of other items for personal care and bathroom maintenance. A simple medicine cabinet may not be enough.

Before you leave the bathroom, check on electric switches and outlets. Are they a safe distance away from tub or shower? Is there an outlet near the mirror for plugging in your shaver or hair dryer? See if there are towel bars sufficient for your family's needs, or room for you to put some up. And try the lighting. The bathroom should be well lit to help prevent accidents. An overhead fan for ventilation is an especially desirable feature in a bathroom.

Attic

Unless you are hard-pressed for space, you probably won't be using the attic as a living area. Consequently, it doesn't have to be a delight to see. Yet the condition of the attic will be more important to you than you might realize, for a good attic helps regulate heat and cooling, provides access to critical areas of the house (the underside of the roof, the ceilings, and the chimney), and offers an abundance of valuable storage space.

See if the attic is adequately ventilated. Ventilation louvers (overlapping, slanted boards set in a venetian blind arrangement to admit air but not rain) should be located in the eaves or at the peak of the roof on both ends. The total area open to the outside should equal about 1/150 or 1/300 of the attic area. The stream of air entering your attic will prevent moisture from collecting and will help cool off your home during the summer. You should also check that the attic is well insulated to make sure that heat will be kept inside.

Is the attic easy to get to? Some homes have a small stairway leading to the attic; others have just a narrow hole in the ceiling. For storage purposes, the former is preferable. The latter type can be reached by a ladder, but you'll still have to do a little dangling and squirming before getting up there.

Some attics may still be cluttered with hard-to-remove objects left behind by earlier owners. Or the attic may simply be too small to accommodate very many of your things—the available space might be largely taken up by heating ducts, the chimney, attic fans, and the like. Such a situation is not to be met with gnashing of teeth—the first purpose of an attic, after all, is to be functional. But a spacious attic does help. Here is where you can store the trunks, boxes, and cartons full of things you don't use much but can't bear to give up. You should not, however, plan to load up the attic with many things that will burn easily.

The best reason for inspecting the attic is to check on the condition of the roof. Since the attic floor will often be protected by a vapor barrier or other covering, you may not be aware of leaks or weaknesses that already exist in the roof. In an earlier chapter, we suggested a walk through the attic to determine the quality of the roofing material; this goes for other parts of the roof too—the rafters, roof boards, collar ties (beams that act to hold together the parts of the roof), and so on.

Basement

A well-built basement can be a real asset in a house.

You may want to make over part of the basement into a family area. This is perfectly practicable (maybe even advisable if your family has a lively element), though before doing so, you should give some thought to the problems mentioned below.

The basement has some advantages over the attic for storage—it is far cooler and more accessible. Even the most cluttered basements should have space enough for some permanent storage.

One thing to check is the location of the furnace. Ideally, it should be placed in a separate room. At the least, it should occupy an area clearly set apart from the rest of the basement. A fireproof divider of some kind will isolate the furnace, at the same time increasing the beauty of the basement. Your own locality probably has regulations governing how the furnace is to be isolated. Check to see what those regulations are.

Look also at the size of the supporting beams. These will have to be strong and solidly in place. A warped or rusting beam has no place in the home you want to buy. Unfortunately, these beams may be largely hidden by ceiling tile or other coverings and thus be impossible to inspect. There is no way to get at them short of ripping away the covering material, and you don't want to do that. In such cases you might have to rely on a house inspector.

There are some headaches that come with basements. One chronic problem is dampness. Any basement you wish to use extensively should be adequately waterproofed. Even then, the air down there may get musty and dank. Since the basement walls must support the whole weight of the house, cracks may appear, letting in more wetness.

If there is woodwork in the basement, it is a good place to check for termites. Termites live in decayed wood. Since they always work from within, you probably won't be able to detect them by just glancing around at the joists and woodwork. One warning sign is a lot of discarded wings around the doorways, window sills, and wall openings. If you see such wings, try piercing some of the woodwork with a sharp tool (like an ice pick). If the wood is soft inside, it is a good bet there are termites.

Look at the cement blocks at the base of the outside walls. A small tube of soil stretching from the ground to the wooden part of the home probably means there are some unwelcome houseguests.

The area between the floor and the ground, where there is no basement, is called the crawl space. You will have no problems with this if you take note of a few simple requirements. Like the attic, the crawl space should be well ventilated to prevent moisture buildup (a ground moisture barrier is a good idea here). If the crawl space is enclosed and properly insulated, wooden flooring and joists will be protected. Finally, the area should be kept clear of lumber, building scraps, and odds and ends. Wood piled under the house is one possible entry route for hungry termites.

Garage

The location of the garage will affect the living patterns within the home.

Its size is a concern. A spacious garage will give you room to move as well as extra space for storage. Lawn equipment, firewood, tools, and materials for repair or maintenance can all be safely and conveniently kept in a garage, leaving valuable room inside the home for more important possessions. Since home ownership usually leads to a steady collection of more and more things, this is a consideration. Naturally, no garage should ever be filled to overflowing.

Notice how the garage entrance is situated. Here, too, size is important. The garage itself may be nice and wide while the garage door is narrow. Trying to squeeze through a car door that is pressed against the garage entrance is irritating, but simple, single-car garages tend to be just wide enough to be usable.

You may prefer a garage that can't be seen from the street, though this feature may be hard to find. This will allow the home to dominate the site (garages aren't generally known for their beauty), but it may also mean a long, long driveway, which in turn means long hours spent on maintenance.

A garage attached to the home has much to be said for it. You will be protected from rain and snow, and the mud from the yard can stay in the yard. Above all, an attached garage is convenient. Easy to get into, it makes a perfect place for storage. Anytime you need a seldom-used tool or other object, you simply step through a door to find it.

There are some drawbacks. An adjacent garage

may be noisier than one that is isolated from the main house. Pollution can be a problem. With car exhaust fumes drifting about, some of those fumes may seep through cracks and doorways. Don't forget that wherever a car stands for long periods of time, black and greasy stains will appear underneath. You may be avoiding rain and mud, but oil residue on the floor next to your home will require occasional cleaning. If rooms are situated directly above the garage, these rooms may be colder than others. Similarly, an attached garage is likely to raise fuel bills by giving the heat an easy escape hatch.

With an unattached garage, the dangers of fire in the home are reduced. Heat loss will not occur because the free-standing home will be fully and uniformly insulated. An unattached garage can be larger than one that is part of the house and can be placed further back on your property, away from the common view. It can even be enlarged later on, as your storage or transportation needs dictate.

However, there are inconveniences. Not only will you have to march through bad weather to get to the garage, but lawn space will be taken up by pavement and garage. In addition, a large structure separate from the house will have heavier maintenance requirements (four outside walls to be cared for rather than three or fewer).

Items to Check

The following is a guide to fixtures and features that too many people skip over or even ignore when looking at a home.

CONDITION OF WALLS

Most walls today are constructed of gypsum wallboard, which, when properly applied and painted, looks like perfectly flat plaster. Wallboard is fire-resistant, unlikely to crack or peel, inexpensive, and easy to install. The sheets of gypsum are simply nailed into place, the seams are covered with tape, and a coat or two of paint is applied.

On all paintable surfaces—wallboard, plaster, and plywood, among others—color and decorating changes are simple. Just repaint.

The things to look for on painted walls are those things the paint can't hide—cracks, buckles, and "pockmarks." Holes or depressions that have been carefully filled may not be too serious; a single coat of paint will restore the beauty of the wall. Nevertheless, very long or prominent cracks and bulges may indicate deeper problems. A heating pipe or water pipe may be acting up, and that means trouble.

You should test wallboard surfaces by rapping on the wall. If it sounds thin and hollow, you probably have the cheap $3/8$-inch variety. A $1/2$-inch surface is desirable; it will keep out the noise that the thinner sheets let in.

In modern home-building, wallpaper is less popular than it used to be. Yet older homes sometimes have papered walls, and some people like to decorate children's rooms, kitchens, bathrooms, and living areas with new brands of removable wallpaper. If you like colorful designs on your walls, there's no reason to rule out this form of decoration.

To determine the condition of the wallpaper, look along the top of the wall. If the edges are curling outward or peeling, old age has set in. Replacement costs depend entirely on the quality of the paper. Currently, a roll of wallpaper (thirty-six square feet to cover thirty square feet of wall) could run you anywhere from five dollars to eighty dollars. And remember, locating a qualified paperhanger may be less than easy.

In some cases, wallpaper could be hiding some faults in the wall itself. If suspicions are raised (by uneven surface or discoloration, for example), look carefully and critically at all walls in the home.

You can paint over wallpaper if you want to, but be sure that the paper is firmly attached and unlikely to peel. Painted wallpaper is very difficult to remove.

CONDITION OF CEILINGS

Check the ceilings for signs of leakage. You are not likely to spot actual holes through which rainwater runs. Look instead for water marks, that is, discolored circular rims that resemble the outer edges of a dried outdoor puddle. Those spots are where the water collects and where it will ultimately drip through.

Make sure that plaster ceilings are in good condition. Since ceiling plaster has to withstand a constant pull of gravity, the weaker sections may eventually crumble and fall to the floor. Door slamming and loud noise will add to the general weakening. Clearly, you don't want a home that will rain plaster.

The costs of replastering or covering the ceiling are fairly high. You can estimate about nine cents to thirteen cents per square foot for plasterboard. Plastering material costs vary too much to make a safe estimate, and labor costs can be high.

MOLDINGS

The moldings, or trim work, are the narrow strips of wood or other decorative material that line edges of the wall. They cover the seams between the wall and adjoining structures (door and window frames, floors, and ceilings) and at the same time add beauty and variety to the room.

Molding is highly visible. See if the trim in the room is painted or stained. In many cases you will want to change the çolors to suit your own decorating tastes, and you must bear in mind that painting them requires bending and stretching as well as painstaking attention to detail. Old, peeling paint also has to be sanded down or scraped off before new paint can be applied. The cost of the paint may be reasonable, but the cost in effort is high.

Moldings also give a clue to the quality of the house's construction as well as to how the previous owner kept the house. The walls may not show too much wear and tear, but at the edges you may find evidence of neglect. The woodwork may be splintered or cracked. Openings between the baseboards and the floor could indicate poor floor construction and upkeep. A stretch of molding that bends away from the wall means the owner didn't want to bother with simple, though necessary, repairs. Nicely painted and firmly secured trim work, on the other hand, indicates that the owner took pride in the home—a pride that undoubtedly reveals itself in other areas of the home as well.

One last word. Some homes have moldings of extremely fancy or involved design. Make sure this type of design suits you. It can be lovely, but you don't want a room that has too many distractions for the eye. It is usually advisable to choose a simple interior design. You can then decorate as you wish.

WINDOWS

You won't have time to test every window in the house thoroughly, but you ought to look carefully at at least a few of them. One thing that should be checked on all windows is how easily they open and close. This is the most common, and one of the most exasperating, window problems. In older homes it amounts to something of a disease!

See whether the locks and handles are in place and in good repair. Older locks may be painted over or may just not work. If the windows lock by means of a metal hook that latches onto a catch, try the hook to see if it moves easily. With modern, crank-operated windows, give the crank a turn both ways. The windows should open and shut with a minimum of effort.

Make sure the size of each window is right for the individual room. Bedroom windows should let in plenty of light, but they should also allow for a degree of privacy. Some builders sensibly place bedroom windows fairly high in the walls to serve this double purpose. Local regulations often dictate the size and placement of bedroom windows. A moderate-sized window over the kitchen sink is a good idea; you'll have more light to work by at the same time that you'll be able to look out the window and keep an eye on the kids. Basement windows will necessarily be of limited size, but there's no reason why you can't have a measure of sunshine down under. Window wells, small retaining walls that hold back the soil from the basement wall, can make this possible.

An important consideration is the availablility of

light. It's not that you'll want floods of sunshine in every corner of your home; in certain areas you may want to avoid glare or heat generated by direct sunlight. In the TV room, for instance, it might be an annoyance. The bedroom is another place where the early morning sun may be an unwelcome visitor. Think of the areas where you'll want light to strike and see if the home suits your wishes.

The easiest thing to determine is the quality of the view. In most parts of the home, this won't matter much, but in the living areas it can mean a great deal. Check to see what the living-room windows look out on and consider your own tastes and desires. Some people like even their living areas to be private, intimate places. Vast, wall-sized windows or spectacular views may not be for them.

If the home you are looking at has storm windows and screens that are not combined in a single unit, ask to see both the storms and the screens. Sometimes storm windows are not included in the price of the home—ask about this too. As with the rest of the house, any prominent flaws or problems should be taken into account when the time comes to discuss price with the seller.

FLOORS

Wood remains the most popular of flooring surfaces. A quick look at the condition of the wood will tell you much. If there is evidence of decay or weakness, a new floor may have to be laid. A floor that squeaks when you walk on it is not necessarily bad, but it may indicate workmanship and quality that is less than perfect. The best kind of strip flooring is interlocked through tongue-and-groove edging. With this type of flooring, a rib on the edge of one floorboard fits into a groove on the edge of another to form a joint. The cheaper variety has straight edges and may tilt upward with time.

If the room you're looking at has wall-to-wall carpeting, see if you can lift up an edge and get a look at the floor below to see the actual condition of it. If it is a good hardwood surface, you can always do away with the carpet and lay a large rug. If it consists of pine boards or plywood, you'll have to stick with a carpeted floor (not the worst of all possible fates). But remember that the costs of recarpeting or laying a new floor are high. A durable, attractive carpet of average thickness (½ inch to one inch) will generally be priced at between ten and thirteen dollars per square yard. A new floor built of tongue-and-groove oak strips runs to a hefty eighty cents per foot. When installation costs are added, the outlook for the thrifty homeowner becomes even gloomier.

Finally, check the quality of the finish. Unfinished wood requires sanding, sealing (applying a protective stain), and adding a coat or two of lacquer or varnish. If the finish on the floor seems largely worn away, you may have to refinish the floor. Though these chores are none too pleasant to do yourself, the expense involved is tolerable.

THAT'S NOT ALL, FOLKS

One problem with examining the interior of a home is that you can't be sure that what you see is exactly what you're going to get. A number of household fixtures and accessories can be removed when the present owner moves out. To help you in determining what's included in the selling price and what's not, we have compiled the following list.

Checklist of Items That
Come with the Home

	Included	Not Included
1. Antennas		
2. Awnings		
3. Bathroom hardware		
4. Bookshelves		
5. Built-in cabinets or shelves		
6. Carpeting		
7. Ceiling fixtures		
8. Chandeliers		
9. Curtains		
10. Curtain rods		
11. Dishwasher		
12. Dryer		
13. Doors		
14. Door handles		
15. Fences		
16. Fireplace fixtures		
17. Gates		
18. Locks		
19. Mailbox		
20. Mirrors		
21. Radiator covers		
22. Refrigerator		
23. Screens		
24. Shades		
25. Storm windows		
26. Tools—lawn mower, leaf blower, and so on		
27. Towel racks		
28. Venetian blinds		
29. Washer		

Simply go through the list with the selling agent and mark all items that come with the home.

For your examination of the home's interior, we have devised a separate checklist. Go through these items one by one and with great care. For rooms and features that are not included on the list, make use of the space provided at the end. Good luck and enjoy the hunt!

Checklist for Examining the Home's Interior

	CONDITION			MAINTENANCE REQUIREMENTS
	Good	Fair	Poor	
Entrance(s) (How many?) back front side basement				
Living room (Is it in a good place?) walls floor ceiling fireplace windows moldings				
Dining room (Is it large enough, with at least two entrances?) walls floor ceiling windows moldings				
Kitchen (Is it efficiently designed?) walls floor ceiling windows				

	CONDITION			MAINTENANCE REQUIREMENTS
	Good	Fair	Poor	
Kitchen (continued) moldings built-in appliances cabinets stove refrigerator sink counters lighting ventilation				
Laundry room **(Is there one?)** walls floor ceiling machines storage space				
Bedrooms (Are they **located away** **from noise?)** walls floors ceilings windows moldings closets				
Bathroom(s) (How **well designed?)** walls floor ceiling windows shower or tub				

	CONDITION			MAINTENANCE REQUIREMENTS
	Good	Fair	Poor	
washbasin toilet counters electrical outlets storage space fan				

Attic (Is it easy
to get to?)
  ventilation
  insulation
  condition of roof
  storage space				

Basement (Is it
adequately water-
proofed?)
  walls
  floor
  ceiling
  windows
  furnace area
  support beams
  crawl space				

Garage				
Additional rooms and features (Specify.) _____ _____ _____ _____				

8

What's Involved in the Contract to Buy?

You've now found the home you want to buy. You've checked into mortgage requirements and loan terms and carefully viewed your personal finances, and you've decided to go ahead.

Having the Home Inspected

Before you start the negotiations to buy, you should have a professional inspector or appraiser check out the condition of the home. (If time is very important, you could sign a contract to buy and make the contract subject to an inspection.) This would be a good idea even if you fancy yourself something of an expert on housing and real estate. A professional knows what to look for and what the various items in your home are worth. An appraisal may well be necessary in spelling out the terms of the deal in legal documents.

A general contractor could probably do the job. If you know of a reliable contractor, or if someone can recommend one, ask how much he or she would charge for an appraisal. Price will vary according to the individual contractor and the nature of the property. The advantage here is that an experienced builder will have knowledge of every aspect of construction from the ground up.

If there is any question in your mind about termites, call an inspector specially trained in finding termites. This kind of work may be slightly beyond a home builder's area of knowledge. And it would be unfortunate, to say the least, to commit yourself to the purchase of a well-built home that is silently being hollowed out from within.

The best idea is to get in touch with a professional appraiser. There are several organizations set up to provide appraisal services. The most prominent is the Society of Real Estate Appraisers, based in Chicago. Other reliable organizations include the American Society of Appraisers, the American Society of Farm Managers and Rural Appraisers, and the American Institute of Real Estate Appraisers. The mortgage department of your local bank or a local real estate broker can also provide names of professional inspectors. Their fees, of course, vary. But this is one investment that is almost sure to pay off. Even if the home is found to be in excellent condition, you'll have the satisfaction of knowing that you're making a wise purchase. If the appraiser can alert you to potential disaster, you should get out—quick.

Some Further Checks

A look at some of the owner's bills from last year is another good last-minute precaution. We've already talked about examining heating and electric bills to get an idea of annual expenses. Find out, too, about last year's property taxes. This will be a good guide to the current value of the place. Naturally, it should not be considered as reliable as a thorough, on-the-spot appraisal by a qualified professional.

If the seller assures you that recent work has been done on the home, ask to see the canceled checks or bills for the work. For instance, if a new furnace has been installed or a new roof put on, don't put your trust in the physical appearance of these features. Ask for the documents. The seller should have them in his or her records.

Negotiating the Selling Price

Now you have to make a deal with the seller. This, unfortunately for you, can be a very complicated and drawn-out process. Here, as in any other area of home buying, it pays to know exactly what you're doing.

The first document you'll be dealing with is a contract that obligates the seller to sell and the buyer to buy. This purchase contract puts the buyer's bid in writing and is generally handled by a real estate broker. To show that you are serious about the purchase, you will have to make a deposit, known as earnest money. This will then be considered as part of the down payment. Normally, this sum will be refunded only if the seller fails in his or her obligations.

Before signing the contract, you should talk to your own lawyer about technical aspects of the matter or arrange for the contract to be subject to the approval of an attorney. Your lawyer will be able to explain to you the terms of the contract. Most important, the lawyer will spot any irregularities or loopholes that could cause you trouble later on. Some attorneys specialize in real estate; it would be a good idea to consult with one of these. Don't be afraid to ask what the fees are. You are, after all, trying to *save* money.

How much should you pay? You should know by now how much you have to spend. The trick is to get the seller down into your price range—or lower, if possible. There is generally some room for bargain- · ing, and you should at least try.

Consider the state of the housing market. All too often these days, this works to the benefit of the seller: outlandish asking prices come together with willing takers. Still, the housing market is an uncertain business, and prices will vary according to region, zoning regulations, changing fashions in home building, the general thriftiness or free spending of the locals—any number of factors. A home that has been on the market for a long time may be available at a reduced price. If homes generally aren't selling at a brisk rate, this may be the time to buy. Check into the situation in your area and see how it can work to your advantage.

It may be difficult to determine just how anxious the seller is to put his home in your hands. Real estate agents can be cool when they're burning to sell, and high-pressure salespersons can seem indifferent when they know they've got a hot property. Remcmber, a professional agent knows his or her trade. However, if the seller is very quick to chop off large sums of money from the original price of the home, you can logically suspect that he or she is anxious to sell. You may get a great bargain this way. Just be sure that it's not the quality of the home itself that's driving the price down.

In some cases, the price will be firm. You can still

make a low bid and see how the seller responds. Some buyers have found to their delight that "firm" does not always mean "hard and fast." On the other hand, it is useless to carry on a one-sided bidding war. If after several reasonable offers a firm price remains firm, it's best to become a believer and simply decide whether or not you wish to go as high as the full asking price.

Through hunting for your home, you will have gathered important knowledge of what particular homes are worth and what you can expect to pay for them. Keeping this information in mind, you can begin the bidding (all of which should be in writing) with a price that you believe is a fair one for the home and the area you are considering. Your first offer may be refused. Once the seller makes a counteroffer, you can either bail out or continue to bid. If all goes well, you'll reach a mutually agreeable middle ground, and the final deal will be in sight.

The Contract to Buy

The agreement should include the following:
1. The sale price.
2. The amount of the down payment. Make sure you can afford it.
3. The date on which you are to take possession of the home.
4. A legal description of the property. This will not be very poetic. It will simply identify the property in legal terms so that there can be no doubt about where your boundaries lie, and so on.
5. A list of any personal property (drapes,

household appliances, carpets, and so on) that are to be included in the sale.

6. The names of the buyer and seller. Be sure that the person who signs as seller is the true owner of the home. In most states, the seller's spouse must also sign in order for the document to be legal.

7. An exact description of the mortgage terms you are prepared to accept. If the sale is conditional on your being able to get a loan, be sure that all details relating to the loan are set down (the amount; the interest rate; how many years you have to pay; whether the loan is conventional, VA, or FHA). If you fail to include this, you may find yourself without a loan, without a home, maybe even without the original earnest money deposit.

8. A reasonable time limit for bringing the transaction to an end and for delivering the title to the buyer.

9. A clear indication of just *who* is to pay for *which* closing costs. Much here will depend on local customs. Get this part straight, since expenses for closing the deal can mount up. Many of these should be negotiated.

10. A statement concerning what is to be done if unexpected problems arise during the time between the signing of the agreement to buy and the closing. If major repairs are made, or if some defect is discovered in the seller's title to the property, who is to bear the responsibility? Usually, the seller is given a reasonable chance to correct the situation. If the seller fails to do so, the buyer can cancel the deal.

11. The type of deed to be used and how the buyer or buyers will assume the title (through joint ownership? through single-party ownership?).
12. Easement rights. These are rights that others may have on, over, or through your property. For instance, the power company might reserve the right to run electric wires over your land.
13. Provision for the payment of proratable items, such as taxes, insurance fees, and rents.

This list is not exhaustive. A well-drawn contract will cover, as far as is possible, everything that may apply to your particular situation. Think about possible confusion or loss. Suppose you are buying a home that is in the process of being built. Who is to take responsibility if the builder's company suddenly goes out of business? Such are the situations that should be provided for.

What Else?

What happens if either party, buyer or seller, fails to live up to his or her end of the bargain? It depends. If you have a thorough and well-drawn contract, everything should be spelled out. In general, you should see to it that the contract protects your interests and makes the seller responsible for delivering the home on time, in good condition, at the right price, and with all legal documents in order. You might want an agreement that says clearly that if the seller fails to live up to certain conditions, you still have the choice of canceling or going ahead with the purchase. This ensures that the seller won't wiggle out of the deal by deliberately violating one of the terms.

Fortunately or unfortunately, the signing of the contract is only the first step in the actual purchase of the home. The final steps are called the closing, which sounds simple, as though all the parties just gather together and shake hands. Alas, it's more complicated than that. To bring the transaction to a final settlement, you'll need to hold on to your lawyer, stay friendly with the broker, and keep your eye on the fine print.

9

How Do You Close the Sale?

There are no rigid rules for home buying, least of all in the procedures for closing. Since individual cases differ so much, no one can tell you everything you must do in actually concluding the purchase and taking possession. Yet there are certain standard steps and procedures you ought to be aware of. If any of these do *not* fit your situation, make sure you know why.

What's Expected of the Seller

The owner has to approach the selling of the home with as much responsibility and caution as you bring to the buying of it. He should be represented by a lawyer in the preparation and consideration of written agreements. If the seller is trying to arrange things on his or her own, *you* may suffer as much as he or she does. A vague, incomplete contract benefits no one (unless you want to get involved in lengthy lawsuits on the chance that you might make a killing—a good way to get "killed" yourself).

The closing is a time for reviewing all the provisions and promises made in the purchase contract.

The seller should be able to supply a current land

survey of the property that matches the description in the contract. You'll want to check out the survey carefully with your lawyer.

Titles and Deeds

The title, as mentioned in chapter 1, is simply the right of the owner to possess and use his or her property, free from the claims of others. As the owner-to-be, you'll want to know that your purchase is yours to do with as you please, without any chance of serious interference. The deed is the legal document that transfers, or conveys, title and ownership.

Title is often transferred by means of a warranty deed. The great advantage of the warranty deed is that it defends your title against the claims of others. In other words, if someone else calls some part of the title into question, you are assured that the burdens of defense will fall on the seller, not you; you are guaranteed your claim to the title. Of course, it doesn't always work quite so smoothly. Should something happen to the seller after the title is transferred to you, the guarantee may not protect you fully. Nonetheless, it's usually a good idea to insist on receiving the warranty deed in completing the transaction. Another type of deed is a special warranty deed, which guarantees only those items set out in the deed.

There are several kinds of deeds, and it's good to know which kind the seller is offering you. The warranty deed has already been discussed. A quitclaim deed gives to the buyer only those interests in the property that are now held by the seller. That means that if certain claims are later made against the property, you are liable, not the person you bought the property from. (This deed may be used in cases of divorced couples where one spouse refuses to sign away his or her share of the home.) If you are offered this type of deed by the seller, make sure you know what the problem with the rights is.

In some states, a bargain and sale deed with covenants, or separate agreements, is used. This deed includes a statement by the seller that there is no defect in the title. In it, he or she is also freed from all responsibility for claims brought against previous owners. Like the warranty deed, this offers you good protection.

A different kind of deed is called a trust deed. This is usually a substitute for a mortgage. The property is conveyed to a trustee, who holds the property as security for the loan. Once the loan is paid, the trustee gives a release deed. If the borrower fails in his or her payments, the trustee can release the property to the lending institution or auction it off. You may want (or be required by your state) to make use of this service.

Though the items that are to be included in the deed vary from state to state, there are some common requirements. The deed must contain an exact description of the property (the same as that which exists in the purchase contract). The names of the buyer and seller must be exactly the names written down in the document. If the property is owned by two or more people, the names of all the owners must appear. The same goes for the buyers—if you and your spouse are to own the property jointly, both your names will be on the deed. Even if one spouse is not on record as an owner of the property, his or her name must appear on the deed. The property cannot be sold unless both of you agree to the sale.

The deed does not have to list the actual purchase price, but there should be a "recital of consideration"—a statement that the property is being sold for at least a nominal sum. Often one dollar or ten dollars "and other good and valuable consideration" is the amount listed.

Not all states require that the signing of the deed be witnessed, but in some states, a notary public has to acknowledge the deed.

As a rule, all the conditions and provisions specified in the contract should appear—in the same form—in the deed. If a mortgage held by the seller on the property has not been paid off at the time of closing, the amount of the mortgage should be included.

The final official act is the recording of the deed. When property changes hands, the designated local official (either the county clerk or registrar of deeds) has to make note of the change in the public records. Be sure to get this done. If you think you've done everything right and then file away the deed without notifying the authorities, you may not legally own the property!

The Marketable Title

A primary concern should be whether the title you receive is "marketable." A marketable title is one that a potential future buyer would find acceptable. Several of the conditions mentioned above had to do with an "encumbrance-free" title, one that has no legal strings attached.

Usually the seller is required to show that the title he or she is transferring to you is marketable. In some parts of the country, the seller must present an "abstract of title," a written history of the ownership of the property. Often, this history is so detailed and complex that special companies are employed to compile the abstract, or put it all together. They conduct a "title search," and the final document they supply tells you what defects, if any, still exist in the title.

Another way in which the title's marketability is assured is through title insurance. The seller usually pays for this. An insurance company can write up a policy that protects you from the most common title problems. However, in title insurance, you get what you pay for. If you are taken to court, the policy will only cover your legal costs if you have bought the type of title insurance that definitely covers legal costs. Obtaining insurance may also involve a title search (the insurance company itself needs some protection).

You should be aware that these guarantees of title marketability may not always be the responsibility of the seller. In some areas of the country, it is you who must pay for the abstract of title or title insurance; this is rare, though, and is decided upon in the bargain between buyer and seller. This is another annoyance and expense, but it does at least give you the comfort of learning firsthand about the state of your property.

Of course, a qualified professional (your lawyer or an abstractor) will conduct the search for you. But when you confer with your agent, you can check on the following:

1. Whether or not there are any outstanding taxes on the property (and whether you will be held responsible for them).

2. If a "mechanic's lien" is attached to the title. A mechanic's lien is a claim advanced by someone (a plumber, an electrician, and so on) who has done work or provided materials for your land or home.
3. Whether or not a "judgment lien" exists against the property. A court judge may have made a decision in the past that went against the previous owner. If so, some portion of the property may be legally bound over to someone else.
4. How local zoning ordinances affect your title. It's possible for zoning regulations to change or to otherwise put certain title claims in jeopardy.

If any of these situations apply to the title you are receiving, get them straightened out. Your lawyer can tell you how. The lending institution that you are doing business with may hire an abstractor or take out the insurance to protect its own interests. Frequently, the question of who is to bear the expense of guaranteeing the title is a matter for negotiation. So ask your lawyer about this. If the seller has to provide for title marketability, check to see that everything is in order. A flaw in the title could turn a great bargain into a big mistake.

What's Expected of You

What do *you* do in bringing about the final settlement? Many of your responsibilities are mirror images of the seller's. In some cases, you will share responsibilities. Remember that it is generally in his or her interest as well as your own that the property transfer go smoothly. Huge corporations can afford time-consuming and costly lawsuits; individual homeowners can't.

You, like the seller, should be represented by a qualified lawyer. It is a good idea to hire an attorney who lives in the area you're moving to. He or she will know the territory and is likely to know the people you'll be dealing with. Such expertise helps.

You probably had your attorney handle the preparation of the purchase contract. Be sure you know how much he or she will charge for helping with the closing. Some special tasks are likely to raise the price of his or her services. For example, in heavily populated metropolitan areas, part of the house you buy may cross over the property line. If such trespassing exists on the property, it must be shown in the purchase contract. For this the lawyer may add to the fee. So tell your lawyer you want to know (as far as can be reasonably expected) what the grand totals will be.

Obviously, you as buyer are also expected to have made specific arrangements for financing. This should have been taken care of long before and written up in the purchase contract.

You may also be required to take out mortgage insurance. This won't protect your investment, but it will protect the investment of the lender, which works to your benefit.

An insured mortgage guarantees that the loan will be paid in full even if you fail to make your payments. The lender can feel confident of the loan and will be willing to provide you with the necessary funds on acceptable terms. The best-known source of mortgage insurance is the Federal Housing Administration (FHA). In fact, the agency was created for just this purpose—to guard against mass foreclosures in unstable times. For the home buyer, the premiums on a mortgage insured by the FHA amount to 0.5 percent of the loan (actually 0.5 percent of each year's unpaid balance of the loan, so that you pay smaller and smaller premiums as you pay off more and more of the loan).

Mortgage insurance can also be bought from private organizations, such as banks or private insurance companies. The cost here will often be comparable to FHA insurance, but it might involve paying the first year's premium in advance as well as establishing an account into which you put some money every month (so that you're sure to make future payments when they fall due).

You may not like paying insurance on your mortgage, but you're going to have to search a bit before you find a lender who is willing to risk a large sum of money on your good intentions. Be cheered by the fact that at least your premiums are likely to go down as time goes on—a rare enough occurrence in our inflation-ridden times.

Finally, if the seller does not supply the land survey (this is decided at the time the contract is made), the buyer will have to have the land surveyed in order to get a mortgage from a lender. In any event, the buyer's idea of what the property includes and the seller's should match. Similarly, their notions of what the property is worth should be fairly close.

The Exchange of Money

What exactly do you pay? And to whom? It sounds slightly absurd, but even the final payment is not without complications.

First, of course, there are the lawyers to pay. They'll let you know what their fees are and how to pay them.

You will be required to pay the balance of the down payment in full. This shouldn't be a problem at this stage of the proceedings; presumably, you will have set aside the correct amount some time ago. This is when you hand it over.

If the seller has paid some property taxes in advance, you will be asked to pay prorated taxes to cover the period of your ownership. The seller can hardly be expected to shell out money for taxes on property he or she no longer owns. This goes for other services and charges that have been paid for in advance by the seller.

As you can see, there are any number of expenses to be borne in the course of closing. Here is a short list of some of the most common costs (including several already discussed).

1. Fee for title search and title insurance if not paid by seller
2. Credit report on borrower
3. Origination fee (in which the lender is paid for various services in granting the loan)
4. Fee for property survey
5. Recording fee (for recording the deed)
6. Termite inspection fee
7. Appraisal fee
8. Lawyers' fees
9. Escrow fee
10. Mortgage-assumption fee
11. Drawing fees (for drawing up the necessary documents, usually charged when secondary financing is involved)
12. Prepaid expenses (including interest on

loans, prepayment on hazard insurance, and
    so on)
These and other costs can be charged to either party
or both. The main thing is to know who's paying for
what. Your lawyer can help you through all this.

What Now?

Your venture into home buying should now be at
an end. If you've taken each step with care and
attention, you ought to be safely nestled in a comfortable, well-built home with reasonable assurance of
adequate financing. The potential difficulties don't
end here, of course. No one makes *all* the necessary
allowances and preparations. And new situations
will invariably arise with the passage of time. But for
now, sit back, relax, and enjoy being lord or lady of
your very own manor.

Checklist for the Closing

HAS THE SELLER—   YES NO N/A*

1. employed a qualified attorney?
2. provided a current land survey of the property?
3. transferred the title properly (with a kind of deed acceptable to you)?
4. seen to it that the names of all present owners appear in the document?
5. signed his or her name exactly as cited in the document?
6. conducted a title search and provided an abstract of title?
7. arranged for title insurance?
8. notified you of any possible defects in the title?

HAVE YOU—

1. located and hired a reliable lawyer?
2. taken care of the financing arrangements and seen to it that they appear in the deed?
3. insured your mortgage if asked?
4. conducted the title search or provided for title insurance?
5. had the property surveyed and appraised?
6. had the deed recorded?
7. found out exactly which of the closing costs you have to pay?
8. arranged for casualty, fire, and extended-coverage insurance for your home?

*Does not apply.

10

What About Condominiums and Cooperatives?

In today's market, ownership of an individual house is certainly not the only possibility for those who want a place of their own. More and more multi-unit buildings are going up, from town houses to apartment complexes, and the chances of calling your own section of such a building home are steadily increasing.

Condominiums, for example, are one type of such housing. A condominium is an apartment that you own outright. There are no questions or complications about title and ownership privileges in a condominium. It is not, however, exactly the same as owning a house. Operating and maintenance expenses are generally shared by the occupants, though heating systems are often made for individual units. You do not own the outside of the building, as does the owner of a house; your ownership extends only to the inner living areas. The lot on which the building stands is owned jointly by all the condominium dwellers. In this, the condominium resembles a cooperative.

The basic concept of ownership is different in a cooperative. You don't really own your co-op. You are, more properly, part owner of an entire apartment complex. This means that you and your fellow tenants all contribute money to the care and maintenance of the building—there is one mortgage, one tax bill. You, together, share the costs of utilities, maintenance, yard work, and so forth. In many cases the members of the cooperative hire a person or agency to manage the property.

Still, you do enjoy most of the privileges of ownership. The apartment is yours for a lifetime (usually with a ninety-nine-year lease) and at an unchanging monthly payment. Of course, you can't sublease without permission from your fellow tenants, but most cooperative members intend to stay permanently anyway.

Condo or Co-op—Which to Choose?

Since the differences between condominiums and cooperatives lie mainly in the area of ownership rights, it is well to give special consideration to these rights. A member of a cooperative is a kind of stockholder in the apartment-owning company and may be under more rigid restrictions than the owner of a condominium. You can't really be independent—just about everything you do with regard to the apartment has to be cleared with the board of directors. The board of directors or owners' council in a condominium complex has less direct control over you.

Are there differences in price? This will depend on many factors. As you might expect, the cost of supporting a unit of your own will be based on the overall desirability of the unit. Location, the neighborhood, the view, the parking facilities, and the soundness and beauty of the structure all affect how much you pay. Sometimes individual units within a single building will differ in price. A top-floor luxury apartment, for instance, would certainly cost more monthly than a ground-floor unit overlooking the parking lot. Similarly, maintenance and grounds costs will depend on the quality of each and may go up considerably. You can't really generalize about prices. Neither a cooperative nor a condominium is necessarily cheaper.

Yet some economic differences do stand out. Condominiums have a higher rate of appreciation because they can more easily be resold. One reason for the comparative ease in reselling is that in a condominium, only the board of governors has the right to review potential purchasers; in a cooperative, every tenant may have a say on who buys a share of the building. Another reason is that a condominium is more easily refinanced. Because the mortgage on a co-op is on the whole building and others have been paying it off over the years, the mortgage balance is low. Therefore, more of the monthly payment goes toward the principal and not toward interest, and a greater amount of equity is built up. For example, co-ops are mostly older buildings with mortgages that may even already be paid off. If such is the case, a banker would not be able to put a mortgage on the building in order to help a specific purchaser pay for an individual cooperative unit. Therefore, quite a large cash investment would be needed by that buyer to reimburse the seller of that unit for his or her equity. The buyer would have to arrange for alternate financing from a bank.

A condominium will carry a higher tax assessment than will a cooperative. However, since property taxes and interest costs are tax-deductible, the condo dweller will enjoy significant tax savings, especially if the property is valuable.

As with all good things, though, there is a catch. Tax assessors levy very heavy property taxes on condominiums. It's not unusual for a person who lives in a condominium to have a property tax bill twice that of someone who lives in a cooperative. This won't necessarily wipe out your tax advantage, but it certainly will reduce it.

One disadvantage to cooperative living is that a declaration of bankruptcy by an individual can result in problems for the other tenants. In addition, some tenants may well be forced to pay for improvements or facilities they don't really want. Perhaps the best advice to give for those interested in cooperatives is this: Try as best you can to get a feeling for the cooperative owner. You will get the chance to literally choose your neighbor.

The Condo or Co-op vs. the House

If your heart is set on a place of your own, you should know that ownership of a condominium has some advantages over ownership of a house. This is not to say that it is necessarily a better way to live; there are simply some attractive features that this alternative form of housing has.

Living in a condominium is likely to be cheaper than living in your own house. This is only natural, since an apartment-sized living unit will generally be smaller than a house and personal ownership will only extend to the inner areas of the building.

Reduced responsibility for maintenance is another bonus for both condominium owners and cooperative members. While the owner of a house possesses and is responsible for the entire lot on which his or her dwelling stands, a condominium owner actually owns only the air space he or she occupies. In other words, the owner doesn't have a plot of ground that he or she must care for alone. All land, buildings, and air space outside the complex belong to the condominium owners in common. Sharing the land and the building means sharing expenses. And this means, in most cases, some savings and a good deal less effort.

You have the further advantage of being protected by your own association board or council of co-owners. The bylaws, which are set forth and voted on by all the owners, will include many details and provisions you might have overlooked on your own. Among them you'll find the following:

1. Rules governing how the grounds and structures are to be maintained and used
2. Monthly charges and assessments
3. Rules of conduct
4. Information on hazard and fire insurance
5. Information on general liability insurance
6. Provisions that assure you that financing and organization comply with state laws as well as FHA requirements
7. A general operating budget

You may feel that some of these rules and regulations cramp your style. You're more likely to find that they provide much needed protection for your investment and your personal comfort and convenience.

What to Look For When You Make the Purchase

The things to look for when you're considering condominium or cooperative living are not that different from the things you'd look for in a house. In certain ways, however, you'll need to see things in a slightly different light.

LOCATION

The fact that you're living in multi-unit housing probably means that you're in a well-populated area. One of the main reasons for such housing, after all, is that it saves land space. Whether in the city or suburbs, you should be within easy driving distance of commercial districts and public services.

Shopping facilities should be investigated. If the complex is near a shopping center, don't just assume that that's taken care of—go into it, walk around, and check out the shops. Remember, this may be the only area for shopping for miles around. If it doesn't have an automotive center or a bank or a Laundromat, it may not be as convenient as it seems. (The condominium or the cooperative will probably have convenient laundry facilities. It can't hurt, however, to keep in mind the possibility of having to go elsewhere.)

Ask about transportation. Very often the new, outlying parts of metropolitan areas are hampered by poor public transportation. Even if you own a car or two, there may be times when no cars are home and you have to get downtown for an appointment. Without adequate transportation, you're just stuck.

As when looking for a house, other local facilities need to be considered. How close are you to a good hospital? to a dentist? a drugstore? a fast-food place? a nice restaurant? If you have children, how close are you to their schools? How many miles do you have to drive before you can take a swim or enjoy an old-fashioned family picnic? Since you'll be living close to your neighbors, you may want to be able to just get away by yourself every now and then. Can you do that there?

The local climate should be considered. If you live in a very warm region, you'll want to know what the rules of the building are regarding use of air-conditioning facilities. Similarly, those who live in colder areas will want to find out about the efficiency and expense of the building's heating system. Ask other tenants and owners. If they have complaints about how the building is heated or cooled, you may need to do some more looking.

Although you won't actually own the land as does the owner of a house, the landscaping will still matter to you. Suppose you are considering a unit at or below ground level. If the land does not sufficiently allow for water runoff, you might find yourself wading through the living room to turn on the TV! Notice also how well the grounds are kept. Chances are that a janitor or handyman does most of the yard work, but you'll want to see whether whoever does the job creates the kind of environment suitable to your needs and desires. Sculpted gardens may be just the thing for you, but if you have kids, there should be a place for them to romp and play.

The number of people in the neighborhood will also figure in your concern about noise. If the apartment you're considering is close to the street, you might have to put up with a certain number of annoying street sounds. Of course, much depends on the nature of the street life. If all seems generally calm and low-key, a location facing the street could be great.

A huge, modern complex of condo or co-op buildings could be spread out, equipped with large play areas, and far from the main road, and still be noisy. Hordes of children or pets can make sounds that will penetrate any man-made barrier. A parking lot that, in late afternoon, is vacant and soundless can become very loud early in the morning. You may be delighted to see the trash facilities located just outside your window; your joy will dim somewhat when the garbage truck roars its approach at 6:00 A.M.

Since condominium or cooperative living involves a large number of people of different temperaments and habits, you'll naturally want to ask yourself about the possibilities for privacy. Find out what your neighbors—especially your nearest neighbors—are like. If they like loud music and late parties, you may want to rethink your commitment. See how friendly the people around you are. You may want to become part of a close-knit community, or you may cherish privacy. A few questions and converstions will tell you a great deal.

Remember, too, that any apartment-dweller automatically takes a calculated risk. Tenants can leave; property can change hands. The neighbor you exchange recipes with today may be in Kalamazoo tomorrow. To be sure, certain stipulations in the owners' or tenants' agreement will give you some protection from various kinds of abuses. But they can never assure you of total and absolute privacy.

OUTSIDE FACILITIES

One of the great advantages of multi-unit housing is that you can enjoy facilities you might not be able to afford on your own. Many complexes are equipped with a swimming pool. Not only will you gain the pleasures of poolside fun; you won't have to go through the headaches of personally cleaning and maintaining it. There *will* be the extra expense of keeping and equipping a pool, but when the expense is shared with others, it won't be such a burden.

The majority of the outside features, however, will be more functional in character. Parking space will be most important. Make sure that you have plenty of space for whatever vehicles you might own. Normally, certain spots will be marked as yours and yours alone. Are these enough for you, or will you need more? Any space in an open parking lot will expose your car to the assaults of winter wind and summer sun. Garage space would be better, but a private garage will up the cost. Sometimes open parking areas are provided underneath the residential areas of the building. This arrangement will shield your car and you from nasty weather but will not protect your car from whoever might wander through the lot. The main thing is to make sure that parking facilities are adequate and convenient.

Check out the walkways. These will sometimes be more extensive than private walkways, but they should be of equal quality in attractiveness and safety. A walkway with cracks and chips may not be an ideal surface for your children to play on. It might also reflect a careless attitude on the part of the co-owners and board of directors toward building maintenance.

Lighting will be another concern. All the walkways should be well lighted. If the condominium or co-op you are considering borders a street, see if the streetlights are bright and evenly spaced. Some modern complexes are lit up at night by specially installed spotlights. This can be very beautiful and pleasant, unless the lights are too bright or are directed toward your living-room window.

Other considerations must be approached in much the same manner you would approach them if you were buying a house. What about the sewage system, the water supply, the condition of the roof and gutters? Ask about the type of waste-disposal system being used. Usually it will be hooked up with the public system. If so, how well does it work and how much will it cost you? Here again, the neighbors will be a reliable source of information.

If you can't see the roof from the ground, go up and look around. In many instances, the roof will be flat and therefore easy to climb up on. Rips or depressions in the roofing should be taken as warning signs. On shingled roofs, look at the edges; if you notice curls and tears, the shingles are probably old and not well cared for. The gutters, too, are important. If they are in good repair and clear of obstructions, the rain runoff will be effectively channeled *away* from your living area. Such things also show the general care with which the entire building is kept.

INSIDE CONSIDERATIONS

The interior will be of more personal concern to you. The living unit you're examining is for you and you alone and will involve an immense investment of money, time, and effort. Don't think of yourself as looking for a comfortable apartment—inspect it as you would a *home* in which you expect to live a lifetime.

Space limitations will make the layout of the rooms vital to your living comfort. Apply the standards mentioned in chapter 7 to your condominium or cooperative apartment. The kitchen should be easy to get to from all areas. The living areas should be separate from the bedrooms, and, if possible, the living room should not double as a passageway. The bathrooms ought to be close to the kitchen and bedrooms and, if possible, should not open directly into the living room. A bathroom just off the master bedroom is a good idea, though many apartments will not have one. It would be desirable to have the dining room close to both the living room and the kitchen.

Test the wiring. Turn on light switches, look along ceilings and floors for frayed or broken wiring, and check the fuse box to see how many circuits service your unit. In older buildings, electric circuits might well be in poor condition and dangerous. There might not be enough amperage for the needs of a modern household. (See chapter 6 for a rundown on the electrical requirements for a typical home.)

Insulation will make a great difference to you, especially since you will be the one paying the heating bills. (See chapter 6 for a discussion of insulation.) Since, in all likelihood, you're not having the unit built yourself, it may be hard to determine just how good the insulation is. The best thing to do is to check the heating bills of the previous owner or tenant. Asking the neighbors might also help.

Of special importance is the quality of the sound insulation. Are the walls thick enough to keep noises from the neighbors out of your living room? Does the insulating material muffle the sound enough? Give the walls a good rap or two and see if they sound hollow or solid. This isn't surefire, to say the least, but it might tell you something. Better yet, ask if you can have a friend enter the unit next door and call out to you. Although you don't want to bother the occupants, it never hurts to ask.

Check out the ventilation systems too. If the unit

is not open to the outside, you'll want plenty of vents for air distribution. The kitchen, most especially, needs to be well ventilated. A place without air conditioning will require a great deal of window space to let in the cool breezes when it gets hot. Even if the unit you live in has air conditioning, access to air vents and the outdoors will be good for both safety and health.

Check all the faucets and the showers for hot water. See how long it takes for the water to warm up. In newer units, you should have hot water within seconds. Turn on the faucets and flush the toilets at the same time to check on the condition of the plumbing. See if the water pressure is sufficient for your needs: If you're located on an upper floor, this could be a problem. Is the water clean and drinkable? Test it and check with those who have been using the water for a long time.

Closet and cabinet space will be another major concern. There may be storage space elsewhere in the housing complex for trunks, snow tires, and the like, but that could be far away or difficult to get to. You'll want to be sure that you can store all the essentials—clothes, valuables, children's toys, articles of daily use—in convenient areas in the home. Most of the guidelines for home living discussed earlier apply here too. A large closet by the front entrance is a good idea. Bedroom closet space should be ample, and the kitchen should have plenty of shelving both above and below the working area.

Be particularly thorough in your inspection of the kitchen. It should be good-sized and fully equipped. You'll need a number of electrical outlets to service all your appliances. The stove and refrigerator should be conveniently located and easy to reach. In determining the efficiency of the kitchen area, think in terms of the triangular arrangement mentioned earlier. The stove, refrigerator, and sink ought to form some kind of triangle so that you can move easily from one to the other. Counter and work space should be ample; you should have space on at least one side of the sink and close to the stove and the refrigerator.

Give the appliances that are part of the purchase a thorough once-over. The refrigerator should be large and modern. If it is self-defrosting, you will avoid annoying and time-consuming work. By the same token, the stove should be clean and large enough for your specific needs. A gas range will do a fine job, though many people prefer electric stoves.

If there is an air conditioner already installed that will come with the home, try it out. Is it adequate for the amount of cooling you'll want done? Many units have built-in places just to hold the air conditioner. Will you want this feature?

In a house you probably would not have to worry about washing machines, dryers, and clotheslines. These could always be installed. But in a multi-unit complex, you'd better give a good deal of thought to the availability of laundry facilities. Are there enough machines in convenient locations? Will you have to wait in line Saturday mornings just to wash your sheets, or can you be reasonably sure the machines will be easily available? It may be that you can install laundry facilities of your own in your unit. Consult the management and the owners' regulations.

Use the following checklist to determine whether or not this particular condominium or cooperative is for you.

Checklist for Choosing a Condominium or a Cooperative

	YES	NO

THE OUTSIDE

1. Are you close to shopping facilities of the kind you need?
2. Is public transportation efficient and inexpensive?
3. Are the roads in good repair and relatively free from congestion?
4. Are there medical facilities, restaurants, banks, laundromats, schools, parks, and dry-cleaning establishments nearby?
5. Are public services readily available? (See chapter 3.)
6. Is the climate right for you? Will the condo or co-op protect you adequately from the local weather?
7. Are the grounds carefully landscaped? Will water be carried *away* from the building?
8. Is the neighborhood noisy? Will this affect your life within the building?
9. Do the parking facilities suit your specific needs?
10. Will there be enough privacy in this location?
11. Is there a swimming pool? Is it in good condition?
12. Do the walkways provide a comfortable surface for walking? Are they well lighted and properly situated?
13. Is the lighting around the building and in the hallways and stairways sufficient?
14. Is the waste-disposal system reliable, and will it meet the needs of the community now and in the future?
15. Is there an adequate supply of clean, drinkable water?
16. Is the roof well maintained and thoroughly sealed?

	YES	NO

17. Are the rain gutters kept clear of obstructions and in good repair?

THE INSIDE

1. Are there enough laundry facilities, and are they easy to get to and well equipped?
2. Is the wiring in good condition?
3. Are there enough electrical circuits?
4. Are the bedroom closets large and easy to get to?
5. Is there a front closet or a closet close enough to the front entrance to hold the coats of your guests?
6. Is there ample cabinet space (in bathroom, kitchen, and storage areas)?
7. Do you have fully insulated walls?
8. Are your walls relatively soundproof?
9. Is the refrigerator of good size? Is it self-defrosting?
10. Is the stove in good condition and suitable to your cooking needs?
11. Is there an air conditioner? Is it large enough? in good working order?
12. Is the living area clearly apart from the working and sleeping areas?
13. Is the living room situated so that it will not serve as a passageway to other rooms?
14. Are the bathrooms conveniently located near the bedrooms and the kitchen?
15. Is the dining area of adequate size?
16. Has ventilation been provided, especially in the kitchen?
17. Is there a plentiful supply of water, especially hot water?
18. Is the kitchen large enough?
19. Do the stove, refrigerator, and sink form a kind of triangle?
20. Does the kitchen have enough counter space?

THE MANAGEMENT

Those who manage the place where you plan to live must bear many important responsibilities. In most cases, they will do their best to handle these responsibilities successfully. Yet you should make it a point to give the management a close check.

First, find out whether the land is owned or leased. If leased, go through whatever process is necessary to find out just who *does* own the property. It is crucial that you be assured that the actual owner is a reputable and stable member of the community. Otherwise you may think you're buying a condominium and wind up with a piece of paper. If anything seems a little vague, talk with an attorney.

If you can, ask who the builder is. Check out his or her reputation with local authorities (public officials, professional appraisers—even other builders). See if the builder has issued any warranties to guarantee the work. If so, you can feel a degree of confidence.

What rules have been laid down governing the use of recreational facilities? The managing board will have some clear guidelines set up. Decide whether these are too strict or too lax for your family's recreational needs. Often there will be regular hours during which certain recreational facilities may be used. Will these hours fit your schedule or not?

In almost all housing complexes, a definite policy toward children and pets will be established. Since condominiums and cooperatives appeal very often to families, outright prohibition of either children or pets is not common (though it is the case in various "retirement" communities). However, if children or pets are allowed, certain restrictions may be enforced. Ask the management about such restrictions. And look around you. In this instance, anyway, you can tell pretty easily whether management's rules are being obeyed or not.

Find out who the managing agent is. Does he or she have a reputation for honesty and efficiency? A personal meeting will tell you much about the kind of person the manager is. If possible, you should find out how long his or her contract will run. If the building is in good hands now, you'll want some assurance that this will still be the case in a year or two.

Explore also the power of the owners' or tenants' association to change the manager. You might select a real dud. If you do, you won't want to be saddled with that manager for a long time. At the same time, you won't want to change managers every time the whims of the association dictate. To attract a good manager in the first place, you'll need to set forth job requirements and guarantees that are fair to all concerned.

In many complexes, insurance on elements held in common will be handled by the management. Find out just what is covered by this insurance and how much it is for. Naturally, you'll want to arrange for your own insurance on the items you hold in your own name.

Perhaps the stickiest problems in dealing with management will arise over your right to sell or lease your unit. This should be looked into closely. If all the terms are clearly set forth from the start, there should be no problem at all. But certainly the managing agent will be affected by any decision you make regarding your use of the living area, and any plans you have should be thoroughly discussed.

Even the condominium owner who is in full legal

possession of a unit can be loaded down with restrictions on his or her right to sell. Some contracts say that you must first offer the condominium to the association for "the right of first refusal." The Department of Housing and Urban Development watches such policies closely.

A GLANCE AT MAINTENANCE

You've already checked out the condition of the outside facilities, but what about the maintenance services? Everything may look nice enough on the outside. The building may be clean, the grass mowed, and the hedges trimmed. But there are certain long-term services that you might feel are essential. It's best to know in advance whether these are to be taken care of.

See about snow and leaf removal. Will walks and entranceways be swept clean and kept clean? Does the management hire a reliable janitor? Which areas are held to be the responsibility of the janitor? This can be found out informally—it's another question you might put to the neighbors.

What about garbage removal? Where do you dispose of your trash and how often do the garbage collectors come? Does the janitor have any duties related to the clearing away of your garbage? (If your unit is not very far from the dumping place, see if you'll have to endure loud noises, exotic smells, or early morning pickups.)

Ask about the gardening. Garden plots on the grounds surrounding the building are generally the responsibility of the management. Decide for yourself whether the job they're doing suits you and whether you want to pay what it costs.

Somewhere along the line, you'll want to go over the management's annual budget. This is the best place to find out what specific maintenance services are being provided for. The allotment of money will tell you how priorities are ordered. Look at the amounts budgeted for roofs and gutters, elevator service, painting and decorating, laundry service, care of grounds—all the services you'd expect in an establishment of this sort. If there are insufficient funds in several areas, consider yourself warned.

Documents to Study

As in buying a house, buying a condominium or committing yourself to a cooperative involves a great deal of paper shuffling, all of it necessary. Don't be overwhelmed. What follows is a brief but useful guide to what you should look for in the major legal documents you'll be confronted with.

These documents are described as they apply to condominium owners. However, the provisions are basically the same for cooperative tenants. Instead of a deed, you'll be studying a lease; bylaws exist in either arrangement.

THE MASTER DEED

The following items will be found in the master deed.

1. An accurate description of the units and the elements held in common. This will make it possible for you to take title and to determine what your rights are to the common elements of the property.

2. An appointment of authority to a board of directors or association of owners.
3. Provisions for professional management.
4. Provisions for insurance policies concerning common elements. These will include fire and hazard as well as liability insurance.
5. A statement of the percentage of interest the owner has in the entire building. This is called the "undivided interest" and determines the extent to which you share in the running of the complex. It can affect how many votes you have in the association, how much you'll be charged for operating costs and taxes, and how much a lender would be willing to loan you on your unit. There are several different ways of figuring the amount of your undivided interest. Find out which method is being used in your case and be sure you're not bearing more than your fair share.
6. A list of common elements that are limited in some way. Parking areas may be commonly owned, but you may have a special right to a certain spot. This can also apply to such things as balconies or patios.
7. The purposes for which the buildings and the units are to be used.
8. The parts of the complex that may be declared commercial.
9. A list of any assessments and special charges. Your share should be clearly stated.

THE BYLAWS

There is some duplication because many of these provisions will also appear in the master deed.

1. A section that defines the association and lays down rules for governing the condominium.
2. A list of insurance policies regarding common elements.
3. A list of assessments and charges.
4. The responsibilities of the board of directors. This will include regulations governing the make-up of the board, its powers, duties, rules for meeting, and so forth. The bylaws should also spell out the board's budgeting policies—its payments for maintenance, utilities, taxes, insurance—and the duties of the managing agent.
5. The responsibilities of the owner—participation in elections and meetings as well as financial responsibilities. The bylaws should tell you what happens in case you fail to make your payments.
6. A statement outlining how the unit is to be used and how it can be transferred to someone else.

The other legal and financial processes you'll have to go through follow pretty closely the procedures for buying a house. The condominium buyer will sign a contract that outlines all the requirements and procedures for bringing about the sale. Financing through mortgage loans follows a similar pattern. The main thing you have to remember in buying a condominium or joining a cooperative is that you're not acting alone. To a greater or lesser degree, you're entering a partnership. This brings its problems and annoyances, but it brings its pleasures too.

11

What About a Mobile Home?

In an age when the cost of a new home can range anywhere from $30,000 to figures in the millions, mobile homes are good news. They are especially popular with young marrieds and retired couples, two groups who often yearn for personal independence yet must work with severely limited financial resources.

Since the end of World War II, the mobile-home business has been booming. For a while the community trailer park was merely a slightly shinier version of the urban slum, an eyesore on the outskirts of town. Now, however, mobile homes can make for gracious living. They can be large, attractive units occupying an honored place in a planned community. The physical surroundings are frequently surprisingly pleasant—landscaped lawns, paved streets, recreation areas, and the like.

The Pros and Cons

No one will try to tell you that mobile-home living is just the same as having a house of your own. There

is always at least a hint of impermanency and imper-
sonality attached to mobile homes. Yet thousands of
people choose this form of housing every year, and a
sizable percentage of them are completely satisfied
with their choice.

THE ECONOMICS

The average cost of a regular mobile home nowadays is in the vicinity of $9,000. Custom-made units
will go into the tens of thousands of dollars. Prices
generally include all fixtures and features—stoves,
refrigerator, bathroom facilities, bedroom and kitch-
en furniture, cabinets, and closets. Naturally, unattached household items like towels, sheets, and
kitchen utensils will not be provided; you'll want to
bring your own anyway.

In the more elaborate units, you'll find all the
comforts of home. These units come complete with
built-in TV, washers and dryers, dishwashing
machines—everything, in short, that you'd find in a
well-equipped home. Often these are found in what
are called double-wides, two trailers fused together to
make for comfortable and spacious living quarters.
Not infrequently such units are placed on a semiper-
manent foundation (the two trailers can always be
detached and transported elsewhere). For a double-
wide mobile home you should figure on paying at
least $15,000.

Though mobile homes are relatively inexpensive,
they aren't necessarily easy to buy. Low-income families may find it difficult to come up with sufficient
funds to make the down payment and keep up the
monthly installments. And costs have risen so sharp-
ly in the past few years that dealers can no longer

always make the claim that mobile-home living is cheaper than apartment living. We'll take a look at the ins and outs of mobile-home financing later on in the chapter.

LOCATION OF TRAILER PARKS

A traditional source of concern for mobile-home owners has been finding a good place to locate. In the past, responsible men and women have had to put up with unethical landlords, restrictive zoning regulations, and insufficient amounts of space. Things are now improving, thanks to the attention paid by legislators and the efforts of honest, reliable developers. Nonetheless, there are snags for the unwary.

Zoning remains a potential problem. Look into local zoning laws as they apply to mobile homes. Many towns and cities do not want to set aside areas for trailer parks, for some of the old prejudices—as well as some legitimate objections—still remain. It could be that the area you're moving to has very little space available for trailers. If so, you may find yourself in something of a bind.

Even if there are parks that can give you space on reasonable terms, the lay and quality of the land may be poor. A park situated in a lowlying area may be a catchall for rainwater and snow. Land that is composed mainly of gravel and sand will not make for a pleasant environment in wet weather or dry.

The desirability of your location will also be affected by the type of neighbors you have. Some trailer parks are designed primarily for retired people. They are located in areas that attract older people for reasons of climate, proximity to needed services, and shared interests and activities. This is perfect if you are a retiree and like the idea of such a community. If, on the other hand, you are just getting started in a job or raising a family, you might want to locate among people closer to your age and situation. By the same token, if you are an older person looking for a quiet and orderly environment, you probably won't be happy in a community of younger swingers.

PROBLEMS WITH TRAILERS

Mobile homes, while excellent in many ways, do have some disadvantages. Many are cheaply made; poor workmanship and shoddy materials are sometimes the reasons behind a "bargain" price. Look for the gold seal of the Craftsmen's Guild or the Mobile Home Manufacturers Association/Trailer Coach Association (MHMA/TCA) seal to know that the home comes up to at least minimum standards. Not all mobile homes of good quality will bear these seals, but most will.

A danger comes in the form of rainstorms and high winds. Since mobile homes tend to be built of relatively light materials and are not firmly fixed in the ground, a galelike wind can cause them to splinter and tip. A hurricane is cruel to all property owners, to mobile-home owners most of all.

DEALERS AND PARK OWNERS

The mobile-home business still has its share of sharpies and smart operators, even though these individuals are now far outnumbered by reputable business people. It pays to keep on your guard. The majority of responsible dealers belong to the dealers' associations in their respective states. If the person you buy from can't show evidence of membership, try elsewhere or at least ask around and find out about the person's local reputation.

The reputation of the trailer park owner might be more difficult to pin down. Of course, the grapevine will tell you a great deal, but you shouldn't put all your faith in it. The best thing to do is to ask about the owner's restrictions on the tenants. If there are indications that he or she stands to profit on a multitude of little items, beware. For instance, the owner might insist that you buy decorating and protective equipment from only him or her. "Entrance fees" might be charged when you come in, or you might be told that you can only resell your home through the park owner. Such schemes are the mark of a person out only for tidy profits. If these schemes are conditions to your living in the park, it might be wise to choose another place.

Selecting the Site

If you've weighed the pros and cons in your own mind and chosen to buy, you'll need to decide where you want to live. This, in fact, should be decided even before you buy the home. You'd better get to know what location is available and whether or not it suits your needs.

The reputation of the park and the park owner will be a major concern. We talked earlier about the possibility of shenanigans involving the managers of trailer parks. Avoid the kind of place that pressures you to buy your mobile home from a particular dealer (chances are the park owner gets a kickback). You can always ask the owner for advice, of course, but any kind of high-pressure, hard-sell tactics should raise suspicions.

Avoid cheapness; that is, avoid the deal that sounds too good to be true. At present, rental on a medium-sized lot averages out at around seventy-five dollars a month. A park may look all right on first inspection, but you may discover, to your dismay, that it turns swampy during spring thaw. A good trailer park will be well landscaped, carefully maintained—grass cut, walkways clean and well lighted, roads paved or at least kept hard and flat—and will offer ready access to utilities and waste-disposal systems.

Much will depend on the situation in the area you live in. Before committing yourself, consider whether the climate is right for a mobile home. In places where weather is severe and changeable, a conventional home may be preferable.

Each state has its own regulations concerning mobile-home communities. Find out how the state of your choice exercises its control over people like you. For the most part, these regulations will work on your behalf. But one person's protection is another one's misfortune. See how it stands with you.

COMPARISON SHOPPING

Your best bet is to compare to be sure. Visit all the parks in the area that might be suitable to your situation. Think of transportation facilities, how close the park is to your place of employment, and your recreation needs; then simply check out all likely prospects.

Observe the composition of the land. Sandy soil

will form gullies and won't be of much use if you're an amateur gardener. A rocky surface might give your trailer a solid foundation, but will it be safe and comfortable for your kids to play on? On the other hand, good rich soil topped with attractive vegetation—be it grass, bushes, vines, or flowers— might require some care on your part and therefore might involve some unwelcome extra burdens.

One of the problems with mobile homes is that once the surrounding lawn area gets a little worn down, the lot begins to look tacky. With a regular home, a well-used lawn just looks well used—as if the permanence of the building lends respectability to the scene. A trailer park, no matter how elegant, usually has a slightly fly-by-night air about it. For this reason, many parks have fairly strict rules governing the upkeep of the grounds. Lawns must be nicely trimmed and edged. Repairs must be done promptly and carefully.

Of course, many of the factors for evaluating property must be taken into account. Look at the trees. Large, stately shade trees will keep you cool and will offer a lovely environment for living. Yet they may restrict play areas available to the kids or cover your plot with dead leaves, cottonwood balls, and other litter. In addition, the mobile home is far more likely to be damaged by falling tree limbs than is an ordinary house.

If the property is valuable, you may have to face a different kind of dilemma. Developers may feel that the land you want to live on is better suited to a shopping center or a housing development. This is another good reason to check into zoning practices in your region. Mobile-home communities tend to have less protection than established residential areas, though this is changing in some parts of the country.

Another thing to look for is the closeness of individual plots. As in condominium or cooperative living, life in a mobile-home community can lack privacy. Some parks are virtually crammed full. This may result in some savings in leasing fees, but it won't do much for your disposition. If you are expecting to live for some time in this particular development, you'll want some room to enjoy the art of living. A close-range view of what your neighbor has for breakfast might amuse you for a while; the novelty will wear off in time.

Finally, there should be parking space appropriate to your needs. A five-by-ten-foot patch of gravel won't be enough for a two-car family. If each plot is provided with meager parking facilities, ask the manager about the provisions made for overflow parking. It could be that the inconvenience will be slight.

A CLOSE LOOK AT THE FACILITIES

If the grounds seem okay, get a reliable picture of the services and equipment provided by the park. If any one of the following items is missing or inadequate, it would be wise to try another park.

Disposal of waste. What does the manager provide in the way of sewage facilities? Assuming you can hook up to a sewer line, how much will you be charged?

Water supply. Since, in most cases, your own trailer won't yet be in place and hooked up, you can ask some of the residents if you could very quickly test their water just to get an idea. First of all, check for water pressure. You should get a good, steady stream of water, hot and cold. You might turn on the shower and the kitchen faucets at the same time. If you're planning on living here for a long time, it's good to know that your water supply will be adequate to all your needs.

Laundry. This is a very important consideration. In the larger mobile homes, there may be room for a washer and dryer and facilities suitable for a hookup. In such cases you needn't worry. But many trailers will not be so equipped. Ask to be shown the park's laundry facilities. Are there enough machines to handle the needs of all the residents? If possible, go there during the hours when you're most likely to do your own washing. If that's when the crowds appear, you might have to consider reshuffling your schedule. Of course, if there's a large and convenient Laundromat close by, you should be able to rest easy on this score.

Recreation. If your family consists of you, your spouse, and a couple of toddlers, a swing set, a sandbox, and a jungle gym may be sufficient—for now. If there are older boys and girls in your household, you should be on the lookout for something more. This need not be in the trailer park itself. A nearby grade or high school will probably have playing fields, playgrounds, basketball courts, and other facilities. A city park may also have such facilities. If, however, there are no public recreational areas nearby, see if the trailer park has at least some wide open spaces for recreation.

Naturally, a mobile-home community won't be the ideal setting for raising a brood of youngsters in the first place. You'd have to occupy a pretty spacious unit in order to maintain an entire family and keep your sanity at the same time. Even if you are childless and plan to remain so, you'll want adequate facilities for personal entertainment and enjoyment in your spare time. Some people may want to locate near a golf course. Others might particularly appreciate a swimming pool or a nearby bathing beach.

Determine your recreational needs and see if the park can satisfy them.

RULES OF THE PARK

Many park managers see fit to enforce fairly strict rules. Get a complete list of all regulations and study it. A look around the park will tell you how seriously the management—and the residents—take them.

Restrictions on visitors are not uncommon. Can houseguests stay with you and for how long? May your guests make free use of the facilities? What processes, if any, are necessary to give them pool privileges, for instance? Can they put up a small tent on your plot for a few nights' stay?

Check for restrictions on children. Some parks—especially those that specialize in providing for retired couples—don't want families moving in. Their reasons are understandable; certainly older people have some right to peace and quiet in a comfortable adult environment. Still, many parks will welcome children. If you do have kids and want to take advantage of the benefits of mobile-home living, you shouldn't have much trouble finding a suitable place.

Provisions for security will be another consideration. Does the management insist on certain requirements in order to keep the park safe? Are there

rules regarding fences, gates, locks, and other security equipment? In most cases, whatever inconveniences you suffer here will be far outweighed by the
extra protection you get.

Other rules might cover such areas as personal
attire, the placement and size of TV antennas, and
pets. This last area could be a particular problem.
Some places will forbid pets but make certain
exceptions—cats may be allowed but dogs sternly
forbidden. Much will depend on the personal inclina-
tions of the park manager. If the print says NO PETS
in big bold letters, you can still turn on the charm and
inquire politely about exceptions.

TERMS OF RENTAL

Above all, find out exactly what the rental terms
are. Some people have a regular leasing arrangement. They rent the plot for a specified period of time
and can renew the lease when that period is over.
Some places still have fairly informal attitudes toward renting, but as business gets ever more lucra-
tive and demanding, such places will have to get
more businesslike. The best leasing arrangements
for you will depend on your exact situation. Talk it
over with the manager, get a list of the requirements,
and see if they fit your own needs.

Obviously, the main consideration is cost. Get a
full rundown on *all* expenses and be sure that you
can afford them. Ask specifically about extras. What
seems like an extra to the landlord may be a necessity
to you and vice versa. In particular, find out how
much you'll pay each month for utilities and to
whom. Electricity, gas, water, and heat should be
thoroughly covered here.

You'll want to look very closely into the frequency and legality of rent increases. You may be staying in this particular spot a long time, and you'll need to be able to take into account expenses for the future as well as the present. For questions concerning the legal aspects of rent increase, ask the housing authorities. If there's absolutely no legal protection from giant rent hikes, ask the park residents about their past experiences with the management. If the past record is good, it is likely that future rent increases will be reasonable. Of course, the property can always change hands, but that's a risk most tenants anywhere have to take.

What are the eviction policies of the management? Do the rules include a section that specifically outlines eviction rights? If you have little or no protection here, you may want to look around some more. Of course, you'll want the management to have some control over evictions—rowdy or destructive neighbors should be subject to control.

Some parks charge entrance or exit fees. Avoid them like the plague. The fees are used only to line the owners' pockets; in most states, they are illegal. Unfortunately, this doesn't keep the practice from being widespread.

How to Buy Your Mobile Home

The task of choosing a mobile home is not a simple one, but it should not scare you. In some cases, your mobile home will be a temporary home, a place to live till your plans are settled enough—and your bank account bulky enough—to allow for the establishment of a permanent home. If you are looking for a mobile home to serve for many years to come, your search will naturally be more intensive and selective.

SEND FOR THE INFORMATION

The first thing to do is to get a list of manufacturers of mobile homes (use the Yellow Pages or contact the Mobile Home Manufacturers Association, 14650 Lee Road, P.O. Box 201, Chantilly, Virginia 22021). Write to each company and ask for any information they have that can help you choose a mobile home. Study the information.

See if the brochures give you details about construction. Many reliable companies will explain just how the mobile home is put together. Naturally, *all* companies will try to make their product sound like an engineering miracle and a home-lover's delight. If you aren't very knowledgeable about matters of structure and building strength, take the information to someone who is.

At the same time, take note of the materials used in the construction of the trailer. This will tell you a great deal about the quality of the unit itself. Items made of finished hardwood, stainless steel, plywood, and brick or stone will be durable. Floors of vinyl tile, ceramics, or oak will likewise be long-lasting and attractive to boot. Cheaper kinds of mobile homes will have thin linoleum, Formica surfaces on everything, and many light plastic accessories. Some materials—aluminum, for example—are used in mobile homes in order to keep the unit light enough for easy traveling. Not all such light materials should be considered negatively. Here, too, it's best to check the list of materials with someone experienced in mobile-home living or maintenance.

Look through the brochures for lists of what is specifically included with the unit. You may see slick color pictures showing a luxurious movable palace complete with plush carpeting, beautiful drapes, spacious easy chairs, and a color TV. If the brochure fails to mention whether these earthly delights are included, chances are they are not.

See if the manufacturer says anything about warranties. If you do find warranty information, read over these sections carefully. What items are covered by guarantees or warranties? Will the dealer help you out in getting quick service on any repair or replacement work that needs to be done? How many years are the warranties good for? Make sure that all important appliances and accessories are thoroughly covered. Air conditioners, stoves, the furnace, the plumbing, and most of the furniture should be included here. A brochure may not go into the details with each accessory, but it ought to give at least a general idea. The specifics should definitely be covered when you go to the dealer to talk about the purchase.

DEALING WITH THE DEALER

The best attitude to take toward brochures is a healthy distrust. Although they can give you a good introduction to the merits and possible faults of various manufacturers, they are no substitute for a personal visit to a dealer.

Shop around before making any kind of decision. Compare dealers. Get a sense of their differences and similarities. Don't let them pressure you.

Be particularly alert to differences in the various sales approaches of the dealers. Is the dealer too enthusiastic about all the units in the lot? Is his or her pitch full of vague generalities, or does he or she offer thorough and clear explanations of the advantages of each model? If you're not too interested in facts and figures, it would be advisable to work up an interest. A dealer who has enough patience and goodwill to answer your questions and give you the full lowdown is worth listening to.

Try to get an impression of the general quality of each dealer's product. Some large-scale operations will offer anything from the tinniest rattletrap to the best and the brightest luxury models. In such a place, just ask for something in the range that suits you. Other dealers will tend to stock units of similar quality. A lot with nothing but small, "bargain-priced" trailers is not likely to have what you want.

Compare terms for financing. Beware of the deal that sounds too good. You'll probably find similar terms offered by most reliable dealers. Determine what's most attractive from the point of view of your own financial situation. Some arrangements are right for certain kinds of buyers and not for others. A good dealer will be the first to recognize this.

Which of the dealers are licensed? If you don't see any sign of licensing in a particular dealer's office, ask about it.

Another useful thing to know is whether it is the dealer or the manufacturer who provides service on the mobile homes. You might have good warranties, but if parts have to be sent in or shipped, there will be long waiting periods and much inconvenience. A dealer who can provide prompt, efficient service is a godsend, though he or she may not have the same degree of skill as the specialists back at the plant.

At each dealership, ask to see a sample contract. This should outline in full all the terms that apply to the sale of the mobile home. Make note of the differences you see among the contracts of different dealers.

Inspecting the Mobile Home

When you actually begin looking over the units in the dealer's lot, you'll want to see how well individual models measure up to the glorious visions presented by the brochures. All new mobile homes will look sleek and shiny. A salesperson's guided tour of the unit will quite naturally point up virtues and play down defects—that's his or her job. So it's up to you to inspect the unit critically. Be on the lookout for potential problems and inconveniences, for flaws in design or workmanship, and for signs of cutting costs.

The brochure probably gave you some indication of construction materials used. Does this check out? Is the sink made of good quality stainless steel or some slightly inferior substitute? Look at the materials used in upholstering the furniture. Are they strong and serviceable, or will they crack at the first bit of rough usage?

Take some time with this aspect of the hunt. Go over every major item in the trailer—floors, closets, beds, appliances, cabinets, ceilings, drapes. Do everything from rapping, tapping, and touching to kicking, stomping, and romping (short of wrecking the place, of course). If you're not sure just what a given item is made of, ask. If you don't know whether a particular kind of material is right for a certain part of the unit, call a builder and find out. In general, materials appropriate to the interior of any home will also be right for the interior of a trailer.

Determine the thickness and strength of walls

and beams. Locating the supporting beams won't always be easy. Look into closets, cabinets, and storage areas—places not meant to be ordinarily visible. A simple visual inspection won't tell you everything you need to know, but it should give you some indication of general solidity. Also apply a little pressure to the beam. If there is some give after just a light push, the structure may be flimsily built.

The supporting structure underneath the unit must be especially strong. Give this a good looking over. The floor joists should be of solid two-by-six-inch or even two-by-eight-inch boards. The lumber should be top grade. Beneath the floor joists will be heavy metal beams. These provide the essential foundation of the mobile home. Needless to say, they should be securely fastened together with thick metal bolts.

The amount of insulation with which the trailer is provided will have to be determined. Some smaller trailers meant largely for summer traveling won't be generously outfitted with insulation. Larger units designed for year-round living should be fully insulated and equipped with a top-quality furnace. You want to stay warm in the winter and cool in the summer at minimal cost. Older people who are particularly sensitive to extreme temperatures will have a special interest in having adequate insulation.

The R-Value, as we've said in an earlier chapter, refers to the resistance to heat flow in the various kinds of insulation. A high R-Value means that the insulation will contain the heat quite well. For a mobile home, R-Values will range from R-8 up to R-20. You'll find that the quality of the insulation is a major selling point for new mobile homes. Since you probably can't get at the insulation to check out the

R-Values yourself, ask the dealer. Some of the more detailed brochures might also provide insulation information.

The condition of the wiring deserves consideration. In a brand-new unit, especially, the wiring ought to be in perfect shape—no frayed edges or exposed metal. Aluminum wiring is nice and light but not good from the standpoint of safety. Copper wiring is standard. If you see several places where plastic seal tape is wrapped around the wires, you should look out—that usually means a cheap and unprofessional job. As a rule, the wiring should be as high in quality and as competently installed as the wiring in any home. Sockets and light switches should be plentiful. All outlets and fixtures should be securely fastened.

The plumbing in a mobile home should be in excellent condition. Pipes made of copper are common, though more and more manufacturers are turning to high-grade, long-lasting plastic piping.

Mobile homes are, by their very nature, unlikely to have elaborate entryways. About all you can hope for is a few steps leading to a door, which in turn leads into the kitchen, the living room, or a small areaway. Yet, you'll want to check out the entrances carefully. Mobile homes are often far from fireproof. Since they are also somewhat restricted as to size, they can fill up quickly with smoke and therefore act as dangerous firetraps.

In a unit designed for year-round living, front and rear exits ought to be provided. The doorways should be large enough to allow for easy, fast departures. Wide entrances will also be good for less dramatic reasons. You'll undoubtedly have reason to move some furniture or heavy appliances in or out during the course of your occupancy. When the weather is nice, you'll want to let the sunshine in by having the doors wide open. Of course, all doors and windows should have screens to let the air in and keep the insects out and storm windows to keep out cold drafts.

Look for plenty of window space. The largest windows are often reserved for the living area. You needn't consider this an ironclad rule, but you can expect it to be the customary arrangement. All rooms—except possibly some of the utility areas—should have some kind of opening tó let in light. Since trailer parks are usually tightly packed communities, all windows in living and sleeping areas should be well equipped with blinds or shades.

Check all the windows for easy opening; this, too, will make a difference in terms of fire safety and in personal convenience.

Financing the Mobile Home

Paying for a mobile home is less worrisome than paying for a regular home, if only because there's less money to worry about. In fact, in many ways your financing will more closely resemble the arrangements made in buying a car than in buying a home. As with a car, the mobile home will probably lose value as time goes on. After about seven to ten years, a trailer is considered to be in the autumn of its years. It can then be sold rather cheaply, like a used car. Some first-class units in high-quality parks, however, can gain in value as time goes on.

Since even brand-new mobile homes are relatively inexpensive, your first option is to buy outright, that is, paying in full. There's no great trick to this. If you've got the bucks, you can get the trailer. Just make sure you've got the bucks.

A more usual method of payment is to get a loan through the dealer. Here is where your experience in buying automobiles will come in handy. The process is basically the same. The dealer gets an installment contract drawn up and sells it to a lending institution. You then hand over the stated monthly payment to the lending institution for the life of the loan. The down payment can be anywhere from $800 to $8,000 (or more) with seven or more years to pay.

The advantages to this method are clear. You avoid many of the hassles that come with home buying—you have to deal with fewer people (just the dealer and the lending institution), and the amounts of the monthly payments will probably be tolerable.

Yet there are drawbacks. When you buy a home, you generally pay interest only on the amount of money you have *left* to pay. In other words, your interest payments shrink as time goes on. In buying a mobile home, on the other hand, interest payments remain the same. At the beginning, the interest on the *entire* amount is calculated. You pay this interest every month as long as the loan lasts. So, in effect, your interest rates are higher. By the time you make your last payment, you may have spent considerably more than the initial purchase price of the mobile home.

In some instances dealers will put together package deals in which certain items or services (carport, lot, patio, and so forth) are included in the arrangement. Such deals may work out well, but they are restrictive.

Insurance on the loan will be yet another expense. Before striking a bargain with the dealer, make sure that you know all of the costs that will be involved in the deal.

You can arrange for financing on your own by going to a bank or lending institution. Regular home mortgages are not available on mobile homes, but loans are. Sometimes the down payment will go as low as 5 percent with seven years to repay. This can lower the overall cost but will increase the monthly payment.

Both the FHA and the VA will insure loans for mobile homes. The FHA will insure a loan for up to $10,000 on a single unit and $15,000 for a mobile home of two or more units. The time limits are twelve years for a single and fifteen years for the multiple-unit models. One real advantage to working through the FHA is the low down payment requirement, which goes from 5 percent to 10 percent of the total price.

Of course, you still have to do business through an approved lender—a bank, credit union, savings and loan association, or finance company. And the unit itself, together with the park in which the unit is to be located, must meet established government standards. Bear in mind that the FHA or the VA is not providing the loan; it is insuring it. But their requirements are reasonable and can be of great help in getting financial backing on decent terms.

Checklist for a Mobile Home

SELECTING THE PARK

	CONDITION			REMARKS
	Good	Fair	Poor	
1. State regulations				
2. Local zoning regulations				
3. Reputation of owner				
4. Rental fees				
5. Shopping				
6. Transportation				
7. Parking				
8. Public services				
9. Medical facilities				

	CONDITION			REMARKS
	Good	Fair	Poor	
10. Type of land				
11. Landscaping				
12. Type of resident				
13. Closeness of plots				
14. Waste disposal				
15. Water supply				
16. Laundry facilities				
17. Recreational facilities				
18. Rules for visitors				
19. Rules on children				

	CONDITION			REMARKS
	Good	Fair	Poor	
20. Security				
21. Rules on pets				
22. Other rules				
23. Rental increase regulations				
24. Cost of electricity				
25. Cost of water				
26. Cost of heating				
27. Eviction rights				
28. Entrance or exit fees				

SELECTING THE MOBILE HOME

	CONDITION			REMARKS
	Good	Fair	Poor	
1. Materials used in construction (Specify.) _____ _____ _____				
2. Thickness of walls and beams				
3. Underneath support				
4. Insulation (Write in R-Value.) walls ____ floor ____ ceiling ____				
5. Wiring				
6. Plumbing				
7. Entrances				
8. Windows				

	CONDITION			REMARKS
	Good	Fair	Poor	
9. Furniture (Specify.)				
_____				
_____				
_____				
_____				
10. Other items included (Specify.)				
_____				
_____				
_____				
_____				
11. Individual rooms and features kitchen stove refrigerator sink bedrooms bathrooms dining area living room storage area cabinets closets heating unit ventilation				

A Final Word

Whether you're in the market for a Victorian manor, a suburban split-level, a condominium, a cooperative, or a mobile home, your search for housing will always lead in unpredictable directions. The standards and practices involved in real estate transactions are forever changing. Exceptions to the rule are anything but exceptional.

So be prepared to make some commonsense judgments on your own. Read this guide carefully and consult it often during the process of finding and buying your home, but don't be afraid to ask questions on subjects not referred to in the chapters. Talk to authorities in the field whenever possible. And, above all, don't stop until you've found a place that's exactly right for you.

Of Related Interest

THE REAL ESTATE DICTIONARY by John Talamo, J.D.

Increase your knowledge and understanding of real estate language. This pocket-sized, 192-page book contains over 2,400 easy-to-read, easy-to-understand definitions of terms related to real estate—terms used in discussion of sales and leasing, financing, and construction.

to order a copy of: THE REAL ESTATE DICTIONARY
by John Talamo, J.D.

write to: Follett Publishing Company
attn: T. K. Washburn
1010 W. Washington Blvd.
Chicago, Illinois 60607

refer to: book title
(THE REAL ESTATE DICTIONARY)
and code number (T0891)

enclose a check for: $2.95 (Price includes postage.)

don't forget to send: your address